DEWEY DECIMAL CLASSIFICATION
for School Libraries

DEWEY DECIMAL CLASSIFICATION
for School Libraries

BRITISH AND INTERNATIONAL EDITION

Revision and expansion of the
Introduction to the DEWEY Decimal Classification
for British Schools

Edited by
MARY L. SOUTH

FOREST PRESS
A Division of the Lake Placid Education Foundation
85 Watervliet Avenue
Albany, New York 12206, U.S.A.
1986

First edition (by Marjorie Chambers) 1961
  reprinted 1963
Second edition (with minor revisions) 1968
  reprinted four times
Third edition (revised and expanded) 1977
  reprinted three times

The 1986 edition is based on Unabridged Edition 19 and Abridged Edition 11
of the DEWEY Decimal Classification © 1979 Forest Press Division, Lake
Placid Education Foundation; published updates and revisions to Edition 19;
and a modified version of *Proposed Revision of 780 Music* © 1980 Forest
Press Division, Lake Placid Education Foundation.

Library of Congress Cataloging-in-Publication Data
South, M. L. (Mary L.)
  Dewey decimal classification for school libraries.
  Rev. ed. of: Introduction to the Dewey decimal
classification for British schools/compiled by B. A. J.
Winslade. 3rd ed. 1977.
  Includes index.
  1. Classification, Dewey decimal. 2. School libraries.
I. Winslade, B. A. J. Introduction to the Dewey
decimal classification for British schools. II. Title.
Z696.D54   986   025.4'31   85–27408

ISBN 0–910608–35–0

Published by Forest Press in association with the SCHOOL LIBRARY
ASSOCIATION, Victoria House, 29–31 George Street, Oxford OX1 2AY

Printed and bound in Great Britain at The Bath Press, Avon

CONTENTS

Publisher's Foreword vii

Introduction 1

Tables 25

Summary of Schedules 45

A Suggested Colour Code for Primary Schools 57

Schedules 61

Alphabetical Subject Index 133

PUBLISHER'S FOREWORD

Dr. Godfrey Dewey, son of the founder of the Dewey Decimal Classification, an educator and one-time editor of the Classification, authorized the first edition of the *Introduction to the Dewey Decimal Classification for British Schools*. Since the flexibility of the Dewey Decimal Classification lends itself to use in libraries at all levels of education, Miss Marjorie Chambers, F.L.A. and School Library Advisor, Derbyshire County Library, was able to adapt successfully the 8th Abridged Edition of the Classification for use in British schools. Her adaptation was published by Forest Press for the (British) School Library Association in 1961.

The two editions prepared by Miss Chambers, and the third edition compiled by Mr. B. A. J. Winslade in 1977 have been well received throughout the United Kingdom. Indeed, the success of this publication and frequent requests by educators and librarians in English-speaking countries throughout the world prompted Forest Press to approach officers of the School Library Association about the preparation of an edition that could serve school library classification needs in other English-speaking countries. The *Dewey Decimal Classification for School Libraries* is the result of the agreement reached on this matter between the School Library Association and Forest Press.

The members of the Forest Press Committee, Walter W. Curley, Chairman, Henry M. Bonner, Richard K. Gardner, John A. Humphry, James M. O'Brien, Thomas N. Stainback, Thomas E. Sullivan, and Elaine Svenonius, wish to acknowledge the assistance and support of the School Library Association in securing the editorial services of Miss Mary L. South, who has broad experience in education and librarianship. Miss South assumed responsibility for the preparation of this edition, which numerically is the fourth edition of the *Introduction* but is now titled the *Dewey Decimal Classification for School Libraries*. The Forest Press Committee wishes to commend Miss South for her dedication to the task and her editorial competence. She approached a difficult assignment in a creative and professional manner.

Special appreciation is also due Mr. Ronald Colebourn, Publications Adviser to the School Library Association, and to Mrs. Miriam Curtis, Secretary, the School Library Association, for their advice and assistance during the preparation of this edition.

Forest Press wishes to acknowledge as well the guidance provided Miss South by the Working Party on the School Libraries Edition appointed by the School Library Association. The members of the Working Party were Mr. Ronald Colebourn; Mr. Joel C. Downing, formerly Director of Copyright and English Language Services, Bibliographic Services Division of the British Library; and Mr. Peter Matthews, Resources Librarian, Balderstone School and Community College, Rochdale, Lancashire, and Chairman, at the time, of the School Library Association.

Dr. John P. Comaromi, Editor of the Dewey Decimal Classification, and Winton E. Matthews, Jr., Assistant Editor, have reviewed and approved the revisions and adaptations. Dr. Comaromi has also assisted Miss South in editing parts of the Classification to bring this publication into greater conformity with Unabridged Edition 19 and Abridged Edition 11. Forest Press is pleased to acknowledge their important contribution.

John A. Humphry
EXECUTIVE DIRECTOR
Forest Press Division
May 1985   Lake Placid Education Foundation

A Note of Appreciation
to John Ames Humphry

John Humphry, Executive Director of Forest Press since June 1977, retired on May 31, 1985.

Much of his time and energy was devoted to expanding the international use of the Classification. His eight years as Executive Director saw the publication of the three-volume Spanish edition in 1980; the first authorized Arabic translation of the Eleventh Abridged Edition in 1984; and the initiation of authorized international editions in Italian, Turkish, Greek, and Icelandic.

John Humphry took a strong interest in the preparation and publication of this edition of the *Dewey Decimal Classification for School Libraries*. It was largely through his efforts and influence that the scope and style of this book have been expanded to better meet the needs of school libraries in English-speaking countries.

This publication is a fitting tribute to his eight years of leadership as Executive Director of Forest Press.

Peter Paulson
EXECUTIVE DIRECTOR
Forest Press Division
Lake Placid Education Foundation

January 1986

INTRODUCTION

Melvil Dewey

1.1   Melvil Dewey (1851–1931) reached a commanding position in
American and in world librarianship during the last quarter of the
nineteenth century. He was a major influence in the development of
libraries, librarianship techniques, and in the professionalization of
librarianship. He is best known for the classification scheme which bears
his name and which he created while in his twenties and a student at
Amherst College, Massachusetts. He also helped to establish the American
Library Association, the Library Bureau (a supply and equipment firm
which did much to standardize library equipment), and the first American
school of librarianship. This school, founded in 1887 at Columbia
University, was moved to Albany following Dewey's appointment as New
York State Librarian. In this post he developed the New York State Library
into the most advanced state library in the United States.

1.2   Dewey was a man of wide interests. He was a pioneer in the creation
of career opportunities for women. In his later years he devoted energy
to the creation of a leisure centre in the Adirondacks, the Lake Placid Club,
which played host to the Winter Olympics in 1932 and 1980. Dewey was
a spelling reformer. Some of the early editions of his classification scheme
were presented in reformed spelling, bearing witness to Dewey's courage
and imagination, as well as to the merits of his scheme, which prospered
despite the unpopular idiosyncracies of its early presentation. As a librarian
and as a classification expert, if not as a spelling reformer, Dewey has had
a lasting influence.

1.3   Dewey's scheme, the Dewey Decimal Classification (DDC), was first
published in 1876. Its influence is based, firstly, on its wide and continuing
use, and secondly, on the innovative features which have become important
commonplaces of librarianship and information science. The decimal
notation, the auxiliary tables, and the relative index have been adapted
and developed (sometimes out of all recognition) not only in later editions
of the scheme, but also in most other successful library classification
schemes. The last quarter of the nineteenth century was a period of rapid
expansion of publication, of rapid changes both in the directions of research
and in the "organization of knowledge." In these respects the period was
similar to our own. The period was, moreover, one of rapid development
of libraries, both in North America and in the United Kingdom; and
especially of public popular libraries, in many of which the stock was being
arranged on open shelves with open access for the public: they were, in
effect, early help yourself supermarkets. In all these circumstances there
was a need for a classification scheme by which stock could be arranged
in a simple and useful way, and which was also flexible and hospitable

1

to new subjects. Dewey's scheme by its structure and special innovative features was a response to this need.

Present status of the Dewey Decimal Classification

2.1　DDC was designed as a means of cataloguing library materials and of arranging them on shelves. It became, with Dewey's permission, the basis of the Brussels Classification. This scheme, first published in 1905, was designed for use in a universal index of recorded knowledge—i.e., for bibliographic rather than shelf arrangement—and is now known as the Universal Decimal Classification (UDC). It is maintained by the International Federation of Documentation and is widely used throughout the world both for shelf and bibliographic arrangement. The main features of DDC are, therefore, known both at first and at second hand.

2.2　DDC itself is also used throughout the world. It is published by Forest Press, the editorial function being exercised on its behalf by the Decimal Classification Division of the Library of Congress. (There is no doubt that DDC's continuing success is in part due to the continuing updating and publication programme.) The scheme is published in several languages. The main subject sequence of the British National Bibliography (BNB) is arranged in Dewey order, and DDC numbers are frequently given in Cataloguing-In-Publication (CIP) data, which is supplied in many publications of the English-speaking world and usually given on the verso of title pages. BNB is now a by-product of the MARC data base, "MARC" being originally an acronym for "Machine Readable Catalogue." MARC is a computer-held bibliography, chiefly, though not exclusively, of print materials maintained by the Library of Congress, The British Library, and other major libraries. It currently (1986) holds records for approximately four-and-a-half million items. DDC numbers are included in the records for most items, and form one of the access points for off-line and on-line searches. The data base forms the basis for a number of centralized and co-operative cataloguing services, which can, therefore, supply DDC numbers.

2.3　The unabridged edition of DDC (in English) is the source and reference point for all other versions, which include an abridged (English) edition. The 19th edition of the unabridged edition was published in 1979, as was the 11th edition of the abridged edition. The 3rd edition of the school-library version was published in 1977 under the title *Introduction to the Dewey Decimal Classification for British Schools* (see Bibliography, Section 17).

The Dewey Decimal Classification for School libraries

3.1　The current editions of the unabridged and abridged versions of DDC list 29,528 and 2,516 classes, respectively. In both cases the number of

2

classes can be augmented by *synthesis*, i.e., the combining of two or more classes. The level of detail thus obtainable is unnecessarily high for most school libraries, and may, indeed, be counter-productive insofar as the users' (i.e., the pupils') understanding of the library is concerned. It is, moreover, achieved at the cost of some operational complexity. The school-library version is intended to be simple for the library user and simple for the library worker, insofar as these ends are compatible with the system's effectiveness. These aims are desirable in all circumstances, but are made more so by the fact that many school-library workers receive minimal instruction in the techniques of librarianship and are allowed little time to devote to the library.

3.2   However, complexities cannot be altogether eliminated if the scheme is to fulfill its purpose of presenting the stock of the library to the library's users. The organization of knowledge which is represented in books and other library materials is, itself, complex, as is the world which it reflects. This is demonstrated by the complexities of curriculum organization and syllabus construction. For example, to decide whether wild life conservation should be treated from an ethical, sociological, economic, or scientific point of view presents problems not only at a curriculum level, but in day-to-day teaching as well. The problems of library classification are analogous. They are aggravated by the fact that such classification must represent a wider and more stable consensus than that represented in a particular teaching programme, if chaotic and frequent changes in the library's organization are to be avoided. Curricula can influence the consensus, and teaching programmes can in great measure change the divisions of knowledge, but library classification must provide for books as they are written or otherwise presented; in other words, library classification must conform to *literary warrant*.

3.3   The mechanics of computer-aided information retrieval may appear to convert library classification from an intellectual to a push-button affair. Indeed, this is in part true, insofar as the input to some types of computer system is concerned. Computer technology makes possible the provision of large numbers of access points to particular pieces of information; for example, a book might be indexed under twenty heads, while a manual system would permit perhaps three. More significantly, it permits the storage of texts (including long abstracts) and long titles that can be searched using natural language, i.e., terms which occur naturally in text or title without special processing for indexing purposes. In some cases every word, and every part of a word can become an access point. The intellectual labour of indexing (i.e., that of classification) is performed, not at the input stage by an indexer or classifier, but at the output stage by the searcher. Such methods are extremely useful and will be increasingly used. They are not, however, suitable for all types of material, subjects, or situations, nor are they as simple for the searcher as might be supposed.

3

They are complementary to, and not a substitute for, more formalized methods. They are especially inappropriate for the orderly display of materials on library shelves.

3.4 This edition of the school-library version may seem to be more difficult to use than previous ones. As the change in title implies, this edition is not tailor-made for United Kingdom usership, but for libraries not only in the U.K. but also in the wider English-speaking world. Moreover, a bias in favour of primary schools has been modified; recognition is given to the fact that the version might be used in secondary schools and in junior college (e.g., sixth form colleges, and tertiary colleges for young people in the immediate pre-university and in vocational stages of education). An attempt to make the version adaptable to varied needs and to rapidly changing curricula (in the U.K. and elsewhere) entails sacrificing some of the simplicities of earlier editions. Some features not compatible with the DDC canon have been removed, partly because these were concessions to the needs of British primary schools, and partly so that librarians can make use of the centralized classification and cataloguing agencies which are increasingly available and can use as well the fuller versions of DDC should they wish to expand the scheme at any of its points. Other changes have been made in conformity with the 19th (rather than the 18th) edition of the unabridged version.

3.5 However, although the school-library version is a reduction of both the unabridged and the abridged versions, it is *not* a scale model. Although it is intended for use in small libraries, because most school libraries are small, there is necessarily a bias in favour of school libraries as such. For example, philosophy is scantily treated compared to minor arts and crafts, and this does not reflect the balance in the fuller versions; more languages are listed in Class 400 (language) than in the abridged version (generally much fuller than the school-library version). Provision needs to be made for the libraries of schools where languages other than English are taught, or where the first language of pupils is not necessarily English. Here, a U.K. bias is shown in that languages enumerated reflect the changing ethnic and linguistic composition of U.K. population and citizenship.

3.6 Literary warrant (combined with the variations in the structure of subjects) accounts for further seeming imbalance in the reduction from the unabridged, through the abridged, to the school-library version. For example, there are likely to be few books which encompass all the "minor arts" which are enumerated in class 700 (lettering, antiques restoration and so on); this lack of literary warrant is likely to be reflected in a lack of "user warrant"—few users are likely to be interested in the whole range. In contrast, works on philosophy at school level are more likely to be about philosophy as a whole than about its component parts. Moreover, philosophy—unlike "minor arts"—is a highly structured and well established subject area, so that component parts can be reliably inferred

4

from a general heading. Teleology inevitably belongs to philosophy, as lizards belongs to zoology. The same cannot be said of antiques restoration in relation to "minor arts." The summarization of a classification scheme is relatively easy where the subject areas are based upon a firm taxonomic and consensus structure. However, many subject areas are not so based, although they may form important parts of the educational curriculum, and in such cases the component parts of the subject need to be indicated.

3.7   For the most part this version conforms to the terminology of the unabridged version, with little attempt made to translate terms to "junior" language. Technical terms are usually more precise, comprehensive, and less culturally biased. It is indeed unlikely that a primary school library would include books on passeriformes as such, but the alternative to the use of the technical term is to enumerate all the species by their popular names, or to make a biased selection of "popular" species. It must be emphasized, moreover, that the school-library version may be used for libraries above primary level, where much of the stock is adult and technical; and that the scheme is not designed for direct consultation by library users, but for interpretation by library workers. The latter are capable of using dictionaries, and the meaning of technical terms is often more easily ascertainable than that of terms in popular language. Examples may, however, be given, especially to help classifiers to recognize a technical category in an essentially popular or juvenile work (e.g., baby animals at 591.3 Animals, reproduction, development, maturation).

3.8   The present edition of the school-library version may be more detailed than is required in many very small libraries, particularly those of primary schools. In the 3rd edition, headings for classes considered to be of particular interest to primary schools were underlined, and the classes were distinguished in the alphabetical index. In the present edition, this practice has been copied and modified. Relevant classes are presented in bold type, and in addition are extracted to form a first-tier summary for use in very small libraries, particularly though not exclusively those of primary schools.

Applications of the Dewey Decimal Classification

4.1   As already implied, DDC is not primarily a search tool, i.e., one that will be consulted by the user when searching for a particular item or class. Nevertheless, it can be used as such provided the searchers familiarize themselves with the structure and operation of the scheme; and it is so used for searches in the MARC data base. The school-library version, which is relatively simple both in structure and operation, might be employed by teacher-users as a search tool; the alphabetical index in particular could be adapted to this end. It must be emphasised, however, that the non-expert user (in this case school pupils) will usually approach the library's

5

collections by means of shelf arrangements, catalogues, and indexes provided by the library workers.

4.2 DDC is designed for classing documents primarily according to their content. The term *document* denotes all kinds of recorded communication, such as books, audio-visual materials, and museum-type artifacts not originally communicatory in function, to which documentary status is given. *Document content* is conventionally referred to as *subject*, and DDC is conventionally referred to as a subject scheme. However, content includes non-subject categories such as genre—works of poetry as well as works about poetry. The scheme is used as the basis for arranging files in classificatory order. A file is any ordered collection of records: for example, books on shelves, entries in a catalogue, information in a computer-held data bank. Classificatory order is an order based upon class relationships, as distinct from one based upon, for example, alphabetical order of class names. By convention only, classificatory order schemes are called classification schemes: DDC is called a *subject classification scheme*, although (as already implied) it deals with non-subject as well as subject categories. Obviously, an alphabetically arranged subject file with cross-references between related classes is as much classified as one arranged in classificatory order, but such a file is usually called an *alphabetical subject file*.

4.3 DDC can be used for the arrangement of stock on shelves, in filing cabinets, and elsewhere, as well as for the arrangement of entries in catalogues and bibliographies. In practice, classificatory order is nearly always used for stock (for shelf arrangement), and either classificatory order or alphabetical order is used for catalogues and bibliographies. By convention, only classificatory order catalogues and bibliographies are called classified, and alphabetical order catalogues are called alphabetical subject catalogues or subject catalogues. In principle both are classified catalogues and both are subject catalogues.

4.4 The advantages of the alphabetical subject catalogue are as follows: The entry terms are usually familiar to the searcher. The order is self-evident, so that direct access to a subject is frequently possible. The catalogue can correct rather than reflect the inevitable "faults" of the classification scheme used for shelf arrangement. A minor advantage is that author, title, and subject entries can be inter-filed in one alphabetical sequence to form the *dictionary catalogue*. The major disadvantage of the alphabetical subject catalogue is that a search over a broad area can be a many-step process since related subjects are scattered (e.g., from animals through vertebrates to elephants).

4.5 The advantages of the classified catalogue are firstly that searches over a broad area are fairly easily accomplished; and secondly, because the arrangement mirrors the shelf arrangement, the catalogue can be used as a stock-taking tool (an advantage especially in small libraries with few employees). On the other hand, separate author/title sequences (author/title catalogues) are necessary, and an alphabetical subject index is a necessary adjunct, entry into the catalogue usually being a two-step affair. However, it can be argued that given a satisfactory (if inevitably imperfect) classification scheme used for shelf arrangement, the classified catalogue is the better choice if there is a shortage of skilled staff. Compilation of an alphabetical subject catalogue entails the use of subject heading lists with elaborate networks of cross-references. These are much more difficult to apply than the equivalent classification schemes; and the process of applying subject headings is additional to that of applying the class marks of the classification scheme.

4.6   DDC can be used for classing all types of documents including those in multimedia collections, although it is not altogether suitable for the classing of live administrative documents as in office files, being in purpose a library classification.

Structure of the Dewey Decimal Classification

5.1   DDC consists of:

   (a)   The schedules
   (b)   The auxiliary tables and other devices for synthesis
   (c)   The notation
   (d)   A first-tier summary scheme (School-library edition only)
   (e)   An alphabetical subject index to schedules and tables

5.2   *The Schedules.* These comprise a list of classes in classificatory order, the order being based on disciplines. Nine main disciplinary areas are recognized, numbered 100–900, and called *main classes*. A tenth main class, numbered 000, accommodates items covering many topics and pervasive subjects that cannot be fitted into any disciplinary area (e.g., general encyclopaedias and bibliography). The ten main classes are the following:

   000   Generalities. General knowledge
   100   Philosophy. Paranormal phenomena and arts. Psychology
   200   Religion
   300   The social sciences
   400   Language. Linguistics
   500   Pure sciences
   600   Technology (Applied sciences)
   700   The arts
   800   Literature (Belles-lettres)
   900   Geography, history, and their auxiliaries

5.3   A disadvantage of discipline-based schemes is that related topics are scattered, and it may be difficult to place items that are inter-disciplinary.

At all levels of education inter-disciplinary and topic-based courses and teaching are common: a lesson in a primary school is more likely to be about water than about any of the disciplines in which water might be studied. Nevertheless, disciplines provide the most generally useful and most stable basis for the arrangement of library stock, and remain as yet the principal starting point for curriculum planning and development. Methods of overcoming problems of disciplinary scatter are discussed elsewhere in this introduction.

5.4 *Auxiliary tables and other devices for synthesis.* Users of computer-based information systems are familiar with the process of synthesis, by which two or more listed classes are combined to form a new class. A search for Agriculture in France is likely to consist of a search for Agriculture followed by a search for France and a subsequent examination of the results to detect overlap. In a computer-based search, the whole process is likely to be actuated by a command of the type "Find Computers *and* France." This method of classing and searching (which often, though not invariably, is based on natural language as described in paragraph 3.3) is in the *post-coordinate mode*: the elements of a subject are indexed separately (under Agriculture and under France) and coordinated at the output stage by the searcher. The method was used before the term *post-coordination* was invented, and before computers were used, although considerably facilitated by computerization. However, it is not suitable for all purposes and circumstances, and obviously is not suitable for shelf arrangement. DDC and similar schemes have as their purpose the production of logically ordered lists of classes, in which, for example, there is a proper place for Agriculture in France between—say—Agriculture in Europe and Agriculture in Provence. For this purpose a pre-coordinate system is necessary, i.e., one in which the elements have been coordinated at the input stage and a precise term or class mark assigned to the whole subject, such as Agriculture in France. Nevertheless, devices for synthesis are usually necessary, in view of the millions of combinations which might potentially occur: hundreds of locations in which a particular activity can take place, and conversely hundreds of activities that can take place in one location. Dewey was the unwitting pioneer of what has become known as *analytico-synthetic classification*: the elements of a subject are analysed (Agriculture, France), and synthesised (Agriculture in France); and in pre-coordinate systems it is the indexer (the classifier) who builds the class and assigns a heading or class number. For DDC the process is called *number building*, because in practice the combining of classes is the combining of class numbers.

5.5 Because DDC is in large part an analytico-synthetic classification, it permits the creation of individual class numbers for a vast number of predictable and unpredictable, old and new combinations; for example, not only for Viniculture in Burgundy but for Growing mangoes in Antarctica;

8

Cookery in India and Food preparation in Space. However, because an item can stand in only one place on the shelves, and because there is likely to be an economic limit to the number of catalogue entries that can be made, it is not feasible to provide for more than one combination order of elements. That is to say Viniculture in Burgundy must be treated as a subdivision of Viniculture or Burgundy but not of both, with the alternative approach provided for by means of cross-references or other compensatory indexing. In most classification schemes, including DDC, the combination order is prescribed (in this case it would be Viniculture-Burgundy), although choices might be offered, as for example Scientists-biographies or Biographies-scientists. In the present work the need for such choices is likely to be limited, and the facilities for synthesis have been restricted in the interest of simplicity. Nevertheless, considerable detail is achievable. Two devices for synthesis are available in DDC, and are provided (in modified form) in the present work.

5.6   Firstly, where there is a specific instruction, it is possible to combine two or more class numbers from the schedules. For example, because it is possible to compile a bibliography on any subject, 016 (Subject bibliography) can be divided by the whole classification. For example 016 + 327 (international relations) = 016.327 Bibliographies of international relations.

5.7   Secondly, the *auxiliary tables* (called *tables* as distinct from *schedules*) can be used to subdivide classes in the schedules. The tables list recurrent concepts. They cannot be used alone or as prefixes, but must be suffixed to a schedule number, e.g.—09 History of a subject, 641 Food and drink, 641.09 History of food and drink. DDC has seven tables of which four are retained in the present work:

Table 1   Standard subdivisions
Forms of presentation (e.g., encyclopaedias), points of view (e.g., history)
Table 2   Areas
Geographical, climatic, economic regions, and specific continents, countries, localities (as already implied location is an important recurrent concept)
Table 3   Subdivisions for individual literatures
Genres and periods to be used only for classes 810–890 within 800 (literature)
Table 4   Subdivisions for individual languages
Phonology, syntax, other linguistic concepts, for use only with classes 420–490 within 400 (language)

5.8   *The notation.* The notation is the set of ordinal symbols (e.g., letters or numbers or combinations of these) used to mechanize the order for purposes of filing and reference. DDC notation consists of Arabic numerals,

9

each digit being treated as if it were a decimal fraction. *Fraction notations*—analogous in operation to alphabetical order—have the advantage that they are hospitable: without upsetting the basic order an infinite number of digits can be inserted at any point between digits to accommodate new classes. Between 1 and 2 as integers no new numbers can be inserted; between .1 and .2 (or between b and c in alphabetic notations) can be inserted .101, .11, .12 ... (bab, bb, bc ...). A second advantage is that the notation can be used to express hierarchical relationships, a digit being added as a *difference* when a class is divided (on the analogy of logical division). It can thus be assumed that the classes represented by 621 and 622 are both subdivisions of the classes represented by 62. (This point is further discussed in paragraph 5.10.)

5.9 DDC notation has two special features which do not affect order or meaning, but which serve to make the notation easy to read, say, and remember. Firstly, a point is inserted between the third and fourth digits. The point is not strictly a decimal point, although referred to as such, since it makes no difference to meaning ($6281 = 628.1$). Secondly, numbers which have less than three digits are made up to three digits by the addition of zeros. However, terminal zeros make no difference to meaning, and zeros are not used *significantly* in DDC notation unless they are followed by another digit. Thus class 6 is labelled 600, and class 61 is labelled 610. (In arithmetic terms $.600 = 6.; .610 = .61$.) In number building, numbers are added to the real, or base, number, e.g., 600 (technology) + 09 history = 609, History of technology; and 610 medicine + 09 history = 610.9 History of medicine.

5.10 *Hierarchies and first-tier summary.* In both schedules and tables, hierarchies are indicated by indention, and almost invariably by notation, as in the following example:

630 (i.e., 63)   Agriculture
633   Field crops
634   Orchards, fruit, forestry

However, the hierarchical structure of the notation may break down because classes cannot always be fitted into packets of fewer than nine. In the following example from sociology, the notation presents as a fraternal relationship what is conceptually a filial one; and in the example from language, the reverse is the case:

301 Sociology   460 (i.e., 46) Spanish language
305 Social structure   469   Portuguese language

In the present version of DDC, indention reliably indicates hierarchical relationships (although this is not true of the unabridged and abridged versions, for which the problems are much greater, and are dealt with by other means). Users of the present work can very easily reduce the level of detail by going "up" a hierarchy from a "contained" class to a "containing" class, e.g., they might choose to class field and orchard crops without differentiation under agriculture at 630. The first tier summary of the classification is constructed on this principle, and it can, itself, be expanded by going "down" the hierarchies in the complete schedules. (Note that classes which appear in the summary are presented in bold type in the complete schedules.)

5.11   *Alphabetical index to schedules and tables.* In the alphabetical index the classes are re-arranged in the alphabetical order of their names, with reference by notation to the place in the schedules where a particular class can be found. The index has a second important function; that of bringing together related classes which have been separated by the classification, as, for example, plants in botany (580) and in agriculture (630), cinema as photography (778.5) and cinema as entertainment (791.43). The index is *relative* (Dewey's term) in that concepts are placed in the context of superordinate disciplinary classes, there being separate entries for cinema as entertainment and cinema in photography. For the most part synonyms are dealt with by means of direct references from each synonym to class number as follows:

Cinema
  Entertainment 791.43
  Photography   778.5
Motion pictures
  Entertainment 791.43
  Photography   778.5

However, if as suggested in paragraph 15.3, additional synonyms are incorporated at the local level, it might be more economical to use a cross-reference to a preferred synonym; any number of synonyms can be incorporated by this method, as, for example, Bioscope *see* Cinema.

5.12   The quantity and nature of the stock in most school libraries suggests the creation of fairly broad subject groupings without subdivision. For example, in the present work the class Primates in Zoology is not subdivided. Such broad grouping presents difficulties to the classifier who might not know that gorillas—for example—are primates, or that wombats are marsupials. The alphabetical index, therefore, provides entry points from many specifics, from "monkeys" to the general number for primates. It is obvious that not all specifics can be represented in the index without extending it to the size of that of the unabridged edition; but additional entries can be made at local level, once it is established that, for example, opossum rats are marsupials. If, as might be the case, the index is used as a search tool by teachers, or as a basis for a locally produced alphabetical index, consideration must be given to the fact that the younger the users the more likely they are to be concerned with specifics (e.g., with monkeys) rather than with general classes like primates, for which they might not even know the term.

5.13   Reference from specific to general is made consistently in the case of the summary scheme. The class number in the summary outline is given in parentheses in the alphabetical index if it differs from that in the complete schedules, as in the following examples:

Criminal law   345 (340)
Labour law   344 (340)
Law   340
Safety law   344 (340)
Social law   344 (340)

In the summary no distinction is made between law and any of its branches, although the distinction is made, and entry points provided, in the index. In the complete schedules no distinction is made between social law and any of its branches, but, here again, the distinction is made in the index.

5.14   The index contains entries for those classes which are enumerated in schedules and tables, but not for those which must be synthesized. For example, there is an entry for German literature and one for poetry but not one for German poetry. Entries for the synthesized class German poetry (830 German literature + −1 poetry, 831) can, however, be made as required at the local level.

Catalogue and shelf arrangement

6.1   The scheme can be used for shelf arrangement, catalogue arrangement, or for both. It is assumed, here, that it will be used for shelf arrangement, as is common, and that it may be used for a classified catalogue as an alternative to an alphabetical subject catalogue.

6.2   In practice shelf arrangement is a one-place arrangement. Catalogue arrangement can be made a multiple-place arrangement, the item being *represented* at each place in which it might be sought. (In practice, however, there is a limit to the number of entries which can economically be made, especially in manual systems.) We are here concerned with subjects only; but in deciding how many entries can be made, it must be remembered that author and title entries may also be required.

6.3   If the scheme is to be used for shelf arrangement only, then one best place (i.e., one best class mark) must be found, since all subjects will be represented in the catalogue by alphabetical subject headings. If a classified catalogue is to be used, then the one best place becomes the preferred place for shelf arrangement and for main entry in the catalogue, additional class marks being found for added entries in the catalogue if necessary. (The distinction between main and added entries is not always important, but serves to show that only one entry corresponds to shelf arrangement, and

that reductions in the number of entries must not affect the "best place."
Two types of added entry can be distinguished: the first usually referred
to simply as an *added entry* relates to the whole item, and the second usually
referred to as an *analytical entry* relates to part of the item. Unless there
is a class mark heading which clearly corresponds to the shelf location,
there must be a clear "shelved at" type instruction in the entry, as in the
examples. Note that in an alphabetical subject catalogue, the class mark
headings would be replaced by alphabetical headings.)

Main plus whole item added entry	*Main plus analytical entry*
943 History of Germany	940 History of Europe
Smith, James	Smith James,
History of Germany and Italy ...	History of Europe ...
945 History of Italy	973 History of the United States
Smith James	Smith, James
History of Germany and Italy ...	The United States in Europe
Shelved at: 943	*In* Smith, James, History
	of Europe, Chapter 3.
	Shelved at: 940

Assigning class marks: content and subject analysis

7.1   Content analysis is the process of deciding what the document is
about; subject analysis is that of deciding what the subject is about. For
example, given that a book is about the American War of Independence,
this particular subject might be considered to be part of the history of the
United States or part of the history of the United Kingdom or of both.
Content and subject analysis logically precede the assigning of class marks
and are logically independent of it. In practice, however, a particular
classification scheme may provide help in subject orientation, and in general
provides the framework within which content and subject analysis takes
place.

7.2   To ascertain the subject of an item it is not usually necessary to
examine it in detail (e.g., to read it cover-to-cover). Such indicators as title,
contents, lists, blurbs, introductions, prefaces, and their equivalents in non-
book materials, are usually adequate. Information derived from external
sources may be helpful, as, for example, Cataloguing-In-Publication,
published bibliographies (e.g., BNB), data bases (e.g., MARC), catalogues
and shelf arrangements of other libraries, cooperative and centralized
cataloguing agencies. It is very likely that such sources will provide ready-
made DDC numbers, which—subject to shortening—are likely to be
compatible with those in the present work; but the information provided
can, in any case, be used as evidence of content and of subject orientation.

For these two purposes, a variety of reference works may be used, and the unabridged version of DDC can be consulted. The highly developed schedules and detailed subject index of the unabridged DDC provide a better terminological and subject guide than the present work, or, indeed, the abridged version; in this respect, the unabridged version is, paradoxically, easier to use than simpler versions. Users of the present work without prior zoological knowledge would have to consult external sources before assigning pongos to the class 599.8 primates, although as explained in paragraph 5.13 many specifics are entered in the index. The index to the unabridged version leads from orangutans to pongos to 599.8442, which would lead to 599.8 (primates) in the present version.

7.3   Subject analysis entails consideration of the topic (e.g., orangutans) and discipline (e.g., zoology, veterinary medicine), and both should be related to authorial intent (see below). In DDC and other discipline-based schemes, discipline takes precedence over topic. For example, although in the present work zoology is the only discipline within which the topic Elephants is specified, zoology is not the proper discipline within which to place a book on elephants as performing animals, which must be placed in a non-specific class within recreational and performing arts. The problem of classing items which are inter-disciplinary or non-disciplinary in character (e.g., "all about elephants") is discussed elsewhere in this introduction.

7.4   Almost invariably the author's intentions are primary. For example, if an author writes about a fraudulent religion as if it were genuine, and believes it to be genuine, then religion is what the work is about, although there is a place in DDC for frauds and hoaxes. Only if the author writes explicitly about frauds and hoaxes would the class number 001.9 be appropriate. Exceptions to the rule that an author's intentions are primary usually relate to the most-useful-place principle. For example, works written in foreign languages might be treated as language-learning materials although not intended as such, and historical source materials may be treated as if they were themselves historical studies (e.g., administrative documents, private letters). In library classification it is obvious that the most-useful-place principle must take precedence over all others; nevertheless, it should be resorted to *directly* with caution. Paradoxically, the most useful place from the users' point of view is often one derived by objective examination of content, with due regard to authorial intent, and without direct reference to the supposed needs of users. This is especially so in the medium and long terms. Short-term requirements are best dealt with *ad hoc* by special exhibitions, short bibliographies, and temporary re-arrangements. For example, an exhibit of books for slow readers may or may not include books explicitly produced for slow readers, and the contents of a selection might change according to circumstances and within very brief time periods.

Assigning class numbers: instructions

8.1   There are generally applicable instructions at the head of each table, the index, and the summary outline. Other instructions appear at specific points in the schedules, tables, and outline. These instructions may be procedural (usually relating to number-building) or classificatory. Classificatory instructions appear only when the class heading and hierarchy do not make clear the scope of the class, and they relate only to those subjects which do not clearly belong or not belong to the class. Such instructions take various forms but all have the effect of "Class here" or "Class elsewhere" instructions. Such instructions include definitions, scope notes, and examples. A special kind of general to specific cross reference is given where part of a subject is treated elsewhere. For example, the subject Nautical craft within Military and naval engineering belongs to the subdivision Transportation and to the subject Naval engineering. At 623.6 (Transportation and other military operations), there is an instruction "For nautical craft, see 623.8"; military transportation in general is to be classed at 623.6; nautical craft specifically are to be classed at 623.8 with other items on seamanship, naval architecture, etc.

8.2   Some instructions relate self-evidently to the class under which they appear and not to its subdivisions. These are for the most part procedural (number-building) instructions, as, for example, at 300 where there is an instruction to use two zeros for standard subdivisions (300.1–300.9). Other instructions relate to a group of classes, as, for example, at 420–490. Others refer to a class and all its subdivisions, as, for example, at 400, where there is the instruction to "Class here comprehensive works on language *and* literature," and this instruction relates also to (for example) English language and literature at 420. The instructions which do *not* have so-called "hierarchical force" are easy to identify, and those with hierarchical force should present few difficulties to users of the present work, for whom it is fairly easy to glance up the schedules for special instructions. Moreover, many of the classes to which the hierarchical force instruction theoretically applies do not have subdivisions in the present version of DDC.

Finding the class number

9.1   Schedules (with tables if relevant) and index should *both* be consulted; the former to ensure that the subject is in its right context, and that special instructions, if any, are followed, and the latter to ensure that all aspects of the subject are considered. Most usually the index will provide the entry into the scheme, but the schedules and tables might be consulted first, if the classifier is not familiar with the terminology of the subject, and, therefore, does not have a specific verbal term to look up. In such circumstances browsing over a wide area may be useful. It is likely that the item will be about one subject and there will be no difficulty about assigning it to an appropriate place. However, in some cases more than one place may be appropriate.

9.2   Polytopical documents are those which encapsulate different works on different subjects. If, as in the case of encyclopaedias, coverage is extensive and systematic, it is usual to class the item by summarization at the class which covers *all* the subjects. For example, a book which deals separately with France, Italy, Germany, Spain, and the U.K. is classed as if it were about Europe as a whole. If the coverage is not extensive, and especially if it includes unpredictable items, then it is usual to choose a preferred place for shelf arrangement and main entry and to make added entries in the catalogue, as exemplified in paragraph 6.3.

9.3   Works on multi-element subjects are different from polytopical documents, in that the *subjects* rather than the physical documents cross class boundaries. A book which includes an article on German literature and another on poetry, does not necessarily include information on German poetry, which is a multi-element subject. Some multi-element subjects are enumerated in the schedules. For example, primitive sculpture, which is conceptually a subdivision of both primitive art and of sculpture (the logical product of Boolean logic) should be classed at 732, but in this scheme it is presented as a subdivision of sculpture. Other multi-element subjects can be synthesized (German poetry is an example). Others cannot be specified, and must be treated in the same way as polytopical documents. For example, it is not possible to specify "Higher education of women." In this instance, there is an instruction to "prefer level" (for shelving and main entry), i.e., to class "higher education of women" with "higher education" at 378, but added entries can be made for "education of women" at 376. Where there is no instruction, an arbitrary decision must be made and noted. It is usually preferable to choose the most concrete and/or the narrowest class: for "harvesting of fruit" to choose "fruit" rather than "harvesting." When consulting the index, each element in a multi-element subject should be considered.

9.4   Cross-disciplinary items may be either multi-element subject items or polytopical items or both, but in practice it is usual to choose one discipline, especially if a relatively simple system such as the present one is in use. Thus an item which contained an article on Anglo-Saxon language and another on Anglo-Saxon poetry would be treated in the same way as one which included a study of linguistic structures in Anglo-Saxon poetry. In some cases (e.g., at 400 and 800) there is an instruction as to where to place inter-disciplinary items. If there is no such instruction, then the most basic discipline in relation to the subject should be chosen, e.g., for animals, zoology might be chosen; for Germany in general, history (rather than economics or sociology) might be chosen. If there is no instruction, and

16

no clear classificatory principle to follow, then an arbitrary decision must be made and noted.

9.5 A special case of the multi-element subject is the "overlap" subject. Multi-element subjects of the type German poetry lie *wholly* within the extension of two or more classes, e.g., "German poetry" is *wholly* part of Poetry and *wholly* part of German literature. Overlap subjects lie *partly* within the extension of two or more classes, e.g., the River Thames can appropriately be said to overlap the county boundaries by which, in the present scheme, England is divided; and nineteenth century U.K. history overlaps the regional periods by which U.K. history is divided. Overlaps occur most usually within the continua of space and time. In some cases (the River Thames is an example), there is a "Class here" instruction which is indexed. In other cases the subject should be assigned to the class to which most of it belongs (the River Amazon to Brazil for example). Common overlap subjects (e.g., mountain ranges, rivers) can be assigned to a single chosen class and indexed. Idiosyncratic overlaps (e.g., U.K. history 1745–1848), may need to be treated as polytopical documents (18th and 19th century). For period and place overlaps, choose, in the absence of other criteria, the early period, and the place first listed in the schedules of tables as the preferred class.

Periodicals

10.1 Periodicals are almost invariably polytopical documents, and like other polytopical documents can be classed by summarization. For example, a periodical in agriculture can be classed at 630 with the use of Standard subdivision 05 from Table 1 630.5. However, coverage in periodicals, although normally extensive, is also miscellaneous and unpredictable in character, so that some form of analytical entry is necessary if the periodical is to be used for purposes other than current awareness browsing. In practice it is fairly common to take periodicals out of the main classificatory sequence, for the following reasons: Periodicals are acquired and discarded in a distinctive way and have distinctive storage requirements. Therefore, for shelf arrangement, periodicals are usually kept in a separate sequence. There are usually few periodical titles in a library (compared to the number of book titles for example); and because summarization is not highly predictive of content (as it would be for an encyclopaedia, for instance), a simple title alphabetical order is often preferred to a not very useful subject order. This does not preclude periodical titles and individual periodical articles being represented in the main catalogue, but the inclusion of the latter (in the form of analyticals) would entail frequent weeding, since the turnover of individual numbers of periodicals is usually high. Separate sequences (e.g., separate catalogues of periodicals and periodical articles) may, therefore, be kept, but in practice there is usually only a fringe need for in-house production of listings of periodical articles. This is because such listings are usually available from external sources in the form of published bibliographies (themselves published as periodicals), and on-line services. Most commonly these external sources use an alphabetical subject system. They may not be available in a particular school library, but can usually be consulted in public reference libraries and other libraries.

Non-subject categories and multi-media collections

11.1   As already stated (paragraph 4.2), DDC is a content scheme; i.e., it provides not only for subjects but also for other features which affect content. For example, DDC provides for genre (e.g., poetry) and form of presentation (e.g., encyclopaedias, periodicals). Relatively little provision is made in the notation for other non-subject categories. This is because in any one library non-subject categories are likely to be few in number and they can be distinguished by letter prefixes or suffixes which can be created *ad hoc*. The advent of new media has added to the number of non-subject categories, but the problem of organizing a multi-media collection remains that of imposing a few non-subject criteria upon a basically subject classification. Distinguishing between sound recordings and print materials within a subject classification is basically no different from distinguishing between periodicals and books or French and German texts.

11.2   Non-subject categories may be storage categories with little or no relevance to users' requirements (e.g., pamphlets, hardbacks) and these can be arranged in separate and parallel sequences on the shelves with integrated sequences in the catalogue. Other categories may be use categories with minimal relevance to storage requirements (reference books, beginners' or advanced books, books in French or German). Some use categories may have incidental storage characteristics (large print/braille/normal print books/gramophone records). The choice for shelf arrangement lies between integrated and parallel sequences with appropriate notational prefixes or suffixes, although the choice may be dictated by storage requirements. Examples: (V is supposed to represent Video cassettes. First three letters of authors' names indicated):

Integrated:	V 620 ADA	620 JON	V 621 SMI	621 TUR
Parallel:	620 JON	621 TUR	V 620 ADA	V 621 SMI

11.3   The choice between integrated and parallel sequences in the catalogue depends almost entirely upon use requirements, although even here there may be conflicts (especially in music). Ideally differences in storage requirements should be minimized, and the packaging of sound and video recordings is tending in this direction.

12.1   There is no provision in the present work for distinguishing between works of and works about music. The former category consists of sound recordings (of more than one technical format) and scores. Whether sound recordings, scores, and treatises are arranged in distinct or parallel sequences depends in part upon storage requirements (for shelving) and in part upon users' requirements: musicologists, performers, and amateur listeners may have different requirements.

12.2   The classification assigns music materials to three main content categories, and there is no provision in this version for combining classes from the different categories. The categories are: general principles and theory; kinds of music by use and occasion (e.g., religious music); and voices, instruments, and ensembles. Church music for the organ must be treated as described in paragraph 9.2, i.e., a preferred class chosen for shelf arrangement and main entry, with added entries made as required. The choice of preferred class depends upon type of material and users' requirements, and whether integrated or parallel sequences are used. For example, the instrument might be an obvious choice for scores (organ music), but type of music for treatises (Church music).

Literature (Belles-lettres)   Class 800

13.1   There is little provision in the present work for distinguishing between works of and works about literature; and no provision for distinguishing between national and regional outputs in more than one language, e.g., for the literatures (in French and English) of Canada. However, national and regional outputs in *one* language can be distinguished by letter prefixes or suffixes, e.g., C 840 French Canadian, F 840 French literature of France. (The prefix might be omitted in the case of a parent or home literature.) Notation 810 is reserved for English literature of the Western hemisphere, but can be used for a literature for which preferential treatment is required. For example, Afrikaans can be transferred from 839.36 to 810, in which case Western Hemisphere English literature is classed with other English literature 820, with or without distinguishing prefix or suffix.

13.2   The literature of individual languages can be subdivided by using Table 3 according to instructions. Table 3P consists of period subdivisions for English literature in general and American literature, French literature of France, and Spanish literature of Spain. French is included as a language of Canada, and as the principal foreign language taught in British schools; Spanish is included as an important second language of the United States. Period subdivisions for other literatures, and other national outputs can be obtained by consulting the schedules of the unabridged version.

14.1   The following is a summary of the geography/history schedules (NB: Geography includes travel):

909   World history
           For ancient world history, see 930
910   Geography. Not limited by place
           For ancient geography, see 913
913   Geography of the ancient world
914–919   Geography of specific continents, countries, localities of the modern world
930   Ancient history
940–990   History of specific continents, countries, localities of the modern world

14.2   The following optional re-arrangements of this class are possible:

(a)   Amalgamate ancient and modern, using modern numbers only; i.e., DO NOT USE 913, 930
(b)   Amalgamate geography and history (except for 909, 910), using history numbers only; i.e., DO NOT USE 913, 914–919
(c)   Amalgamate ancient geography and ancient history, using history numbers only; i.e., DO NOT USE 913
(d)   Amalgamate geography and history (except for 909, 910), and ancient and modern, using modern history numbers only; i.e., DO NOT USE 913, 914–919, 930

Amalgamations can be selective; for example, the distinction between ancient and modern can be made for Greece and Rome but not for Britain.
14.3   Period subdivisions in history are given for some areas only. Extensions of these subdivisions and subdivisions for other areas can be obtained from the schedules of the unabridged version.

Adapting and maintaining the scheme

15.1   The scheme can be extended at any point by borrowing numbers from the unabridged or abridged versions. This is likely to be useful in the case of highly enumerative classes, which generate a large number of logically equal, and—local interests aside—equally important sub-classes, e.g., species in zoology, languages in the language class, places in Table 2, and specific religions in the religion class.
15.2   The scheme can be abbreviated by going up the hierarchies to a more general class. For example, one can ignore all subdivisions for mathematics, classing all branches without distinction at 510. However, a ready-made abbreviation has been provided in the summary, which can be used

selectively, and which can itself be extended, according to instructions given at the head of the summary.

15.3 Additional index entries can be made for synonyms and specifics, as explained in paragraph 5.11, and also for overlap subjects, at which a class here instruction should be given in addition to the index entry (see paragraph 9.5). Additional synonyms may be especially useful in respect of local usage and popular terminology; for example, "Living together" might in some circumstances be a synonym for "sociology." It may be useful, but not always necessary, to make index entries for newly synthesized classes (e.g., for Italian poetry) the first time the number (851) is used. Such additional entries may become necessary if, as suggested in paragraph 4.1, the index is used by library users or if there are frequent changes in library staff.

15.4 All extensions, abbreviations, choice of options, and amendments should be noted as appropriate in schedules, tables, index, and summary.

Class numbers: Samples (Class numbers for summary in parentheses)

16.1 *Simple index to schedules search*
Education 370 (370)

16.2 *Use of Table 1*
History of Education 370 + 09 = 370.9 (370)
History of engineering 620 + 009 = 620.09 (620)

16.3 *Use of Table 1 with Table 2*
History of Education in China 370 + 09 + 51 = 370.951 (370)
Engineering in China 620 + 009 + 51 = 620.0951 (620)

16.4 *Use of Table 2 without Table 1*
Christianity in Asia 270 + 5 = 275 (270)

16.5 *Use of Table 3*
German drama 830 + 2 = 832 (830)

16.6 *Use of Table 3P*
Victorian English poetry 821 + 8 = 821.8 (821)

16.7 *Inter-disciplinary items*
Handbook of Italian language and literature 450 (450)
Handbook of Italian life and culture 945 (945)

16.8 *Combining numbers from schedules*
Bibliography of medicine 016 + 610 = 016.61 (011)

16.9 *Non-specifiable subjects*
Poetry of the Romance languages 840 (840)
(Class number represents literature in general of the Romance languages)

21

Italian poetry of the later sixteenth century 851 (850)
(Class number relates to Italian poetry in general. However, period numbers available from unabridged version)

Growing tulips in the garden 635.9 (635.9)
(Class number relates to flower gardening in general)

Cooking and table service 641.5 (641.5)
(Class number relates to cooking. Added entry at 642 table service possible [not in summary.])

Bibliography

17.1 Dewey, Melvil 1851–1931
Dewey Decimal Classification and Relative Index. Devised by Melvil Dewey. 19th ed., edited under the direction of Benjamin A. Custer. 3 vols. Albany, New York: Forest Press, 1979. (The unabridged version.)

17.2 Dewey, Melvil 1851–1931
Abridged Dewey Decimal Classification and Relative Index. Devised by Melvil Dewey. 11th ed., edited under the direction of Benjamin A. Custer. Albany, New York: Forest Press, 1979. (The abridged version.)

17.3 *Introduction to the Dewey Decimal Classification for British Schools*. 3rd ed., compiled by B. A. J. Winslade. Albany, New York: Forest Press, for School Library Association (Oxford, England), 1977. (First edition, 1961 by Marjorie Chambers. The school-library version.)

Tables

TABLES

Table 1 Standard Subdivisions

   The following numbers are never used alone or as prefixes. Unless contrary instructions are given they may be added as suffixes to the base numbers of classes in the schedules. The base numbers are the same as the class numbers with terminal zeros (if any) deleted. A point is inserted between the third and fourth digits. Examples: encyclopaedias (—03 in this table) of technology (600, i.e., 6), 603; of medicine (610, i.e., 61), 610.3; of human physiology and anatomy (612), 612.03. Subdivisions are usually introduced by a single zero to form the notational series 01–09. However, two zeros are used (001–009) if the 01–09 series is pre-empted for other purposes. Examples: study and teaching (—07 in this table) of the social sciences (300, i.e., 3), 300.7; of engineering (620, i.e., 62), 620.07, rather than 307 and 620.7, because these numbers respectively mean "communities" within sociology, and "systems engineering." A reminder of the two-zero rule is given wherever standard subdivisions are likely to be needed, as at 300 and 620, but not otherwise. Special applications of numbers in this table are given at appropriate points in the schedules as at 780.7 where the standard subdivision Study and teaching includes "performances, festivals, competitions, awards."

   The table may be used in its entirety (i.e., *all* the numbers in the table are used) and non-selectively for classes in the schedules (i.e., the numbers will be applied wherever they are relevant). On the other hand, it may be used selectively for either numbers in the tables or in the schedules or both. For example, it might be decided to use only —09 history, and to apply it wherever the "history" concept appears; or it might be decided to use the whole series but only for main classes, e.g., encyclopaedias, history, study and teaching, etc. of technology but not of any of its branches. The table need not be used at all, and should preferably not be used with the summary schedules.

—01	Philosophy and theory
—016	Indexes, bibliographies, catalogues
—019	Psychological principles
—02	Miscellany
—020 8	Audiovisual treatment
—022	Illustrations and models
	Pictures, charts, designs, plans, diagrams, drafting illustrations, and other illustrations
—023	The subject as a profession, occupation, hobby

—025	Directories of persons and organizations
—028	Techniques, procedures, apparatus, equipment, materials, data processing
—029	Commercial catalogues, price lists
—03	Dictionaries, encyclopaedias, concordances
—05	Serial publications
	Examples: annuals, yearbooks, periodicals
—06	Management and organizations
	Management principles and techniques with respect to the subject. History, description, membership lists of organizations
—07	Study and teaching
	Class study and teaching at the elementary level in 372 (schedules)
—074	Museums, collections, exhibitions
—075	Collecting objects
—09	Historical and geographical treatment
	Before applying this number, check that historical and geographical treatment is not otherwise provided for (as at 270, history of Christianity)
—091	Treatment by areas, regions, places in general
	Not limited by continent, country, locality. Add "Areas" notation 1 from Table 2 to base number 09, e.g., agriculture in the tropics, 630 (i.e., 63) + 09 + 13, 630.913. However, see note at 09
—092	Persons associated with the subject
	Example: Lives of agriculturalists, 630.92. If preferred, class in 920
—093–099	Treatment by specific continents, countries, localities; extraterrestrial worlds
	Add "Areas" notation 3–9 from Table 2 to base number —09, e.g., agriculture in Italy, 630 (i.e., 63) + 09 + 45, 630.945; housing in Italy, 363.50945. However, see note at 09

Table 2   Areas

The following numbers are never used alone or as prefixes. They may be added as suffixes to base numbers of classes in the schedules according to instructions in specific places in the schedules, e.g., at 274–279. Where there are no instructions they may be used through the interposition of "Standard subdivision" —09 from Table 1. See instructions for Table 1 and examples at —091 and —093–099. A point is inserted between the third and fourth digits. This table may be used selectively or not at all, as explained for Table 1.

—1	Areas, regions, places in general
	Not limited by continent, country, locality
—11	Frigid zones
—12	Temperate zones
—13	Torrid zones (Tropics)
—14	Land and land forms
—141	Continents and continental shelves
—142	Islands
—143	Mountains, hills, plateaus
—144	Valleys, canyons, caves
—145	Plane regions
	Examples: prairies, pampas, steppes
—146	Coastal regions and shore lines
—15	Regions by type of vegetation
—152	Forests
—153	Grasslands
—154	Deserts
—16	Air and water
—161	Atmosphere
—162	Oceans and seas
—163	Atlantic Ocean
	For Antarctic waters, see —167
—163 2	Arctic Ocean (North Polar Sea)
—163 8	Mediterranean Sea
—164	Pacific Ocean
	For Antarctic waters, see —167
—165	Indian Ocean
	For Antarctic waters, see —167
—167	Antarctic waters
—169	Fresh and brackish waters
	Examples: rivers, lakes

—17	Socioeconomic regions
—171	By political orientation
—171 2	Non-contiguous political unions and empires

—17   Socioeconomic regions
—171   By political orientation
—171 2   Non-contiguous political unions and empires
        Add "Areas" notation 3–9 to base number 1712 for
        "mother" country, e.g., The French community
        —171244; the (former) British Commonwealth—17124

—171 3   Western bloc
—171 6   Unaligned blocs
—171 7   Eastern bloc
—172   By degree of economic development
        High, medium, low
—173   By concentration of population
—173 2   Urban and suburban areas
—173 4   Rural areas
—18   Other kinds of terrestrial regions
—181   Hemispheres
—181 1   Eastern
—181 2   Western
—181 3   Northern
—181 4   Southern
—182   Ocean and sea basins
        The totality of land facing, and islands in, major bodies
        of water. For oceans and seas, see —16
—182 1   Atlantic region. Occident
—182 2   Mediterranean region
—182 3   Pacific region
—182 4   Indian Ocean region
—19   Space
—3   The ancient world
—31   China
—32   Egypt
—33   Palestine
—34   India
—35   Mesopotamia and the Iranian plateau
—36   Europe north and west of the Italian peninsula
—361   British Isles
—363   Germanic regions
        For British Isles, see —361
—364   Celtic regions
        For British Isles, see —361
—366   Iberian peninsula and adjacent islands
—37   Italian peninsula and adjacent islands
        Class here Roman empire. For comprehensive works on
        ancient Greece and Rome, see —38

—38   Greece
           Class here comprehensive works on ancient Greece and
           Rome; the Hellenic empire
—39   Other parts of the ancient world
—4–9   The modern world. Extraterrestrial worlds
—4   Europe
           Class here comprehensive works on Western Europe
—41   The British Isles, United Kingdom, Great Britain
—411   Scotland
—411 1   Northern Scotland
               Class here Northern Scotland in general and the Scottish
               highlands and islands. For Northeastern Scotland, see—412
—412   Northeastern Scotland
               Fife, Grampian, Tayside regions
—413   Southeastern Scotland
               Borders, Central, Lothian regions
—413 4   Edinburgh district
—414   Southwestern Scotland
               Dumfries and Galloway, Strathclyde regions
—415   Ireland
           For Eire, see 417
—416   Ulster. Northern Ireland
—416 1   Northeast area
                   Antrim, Ballymena, Ballymoney, Carrickfergus,
                   Larne, Lisburn, Moyle, Newtonabbey
—416 2   Western area
                   Coleraine, Cookstown, Derry (Londonderry),
                   Dunganon, Fermanagh, Limavady, Magherafelt,
                   Omagh, Strabane. Class here former County
                   Tyrone
—416 5   Southeast area
                   Ards, Banbridge, Castlreagh, Down, Newry and
                   Mourne, North Down
—416 6   Southern area
                   Armagh, Craigavon
—416 7   Belfast district
—416 9   Counties of Republic of Ireland in Ulster
                   Cavan, Donegal, Monaghan
—417   Eire (Republic of Ireland)
               For counties of Republic in Ulster, see —4169
—417 1   Connacht
—418   Leinster
—418 3   Dublin (County and City)
—419   Munster

29

—42	England, Wales, Isle of Man, Channel Islands
	For Channel Islands, see —4234; Isle of Man, —4279; Wales, —429
—421	Greater London
—422	Southeastern England
	Berkshire, East Sussex, Hampshire, Isle of Wight, Kent, Surrey, West Sussex. Class here Home Counties, River Thames. For Greater London, see —421
—423	Southwestern England and the Channel Islands
	Avon, Cornwall, Devon, Dorset, Scilly Isles, Somerset, Wiltshire
—423 4	Channel Islands
—424	Midlands
	Gloucestershire, Hereford and Worcester, Shropshire, Staffordshire, Warwickshire, West Midlands (County). For East Midlands, see —425
—425	East Midlands
	Bedfordshire, Buckinghamshire, Derbyshire, Hertfordshire, Leicestershire, Lincolnshire, Northamptonshire, Nottinghamshire, Oxfordshire
—426	Eastern England
	Cambridgeshire, Essex, Norfolk, Suffolk. Class here East Anglia
—427	Northwestern England and the Isle of Man
	Cheshire, Cumbria, Greater Manchester, Lancashire, Merseyside (County). Class here Northern England, the North Country. For Northeastern England, see —428
—427 9	Isle of Man
—428	Northeastern England
	Cleveland, Durham, Humberside, North Yorkshire, Northumberland, South Yorkshire (County), West Yorkshire (County), Tyne and Wear (County). For Northern England in general, see —427
—429	Wales
—429 1	North Wales
	Gwynedd, Clwyd
—429 2	South Wales
	Dyfed, Glamorgan, Gwent, Powys
—43	Germany
	Class here, without subdivision, Central Europe in general, Holy Roman Empire

—431	German Democratic Republic
—431 5	Berlin
—433	Federal Republic of Germany
—436	Austria and Lichtenstein
—437	Czechoslovakia
—438	Poland
—439	Hungary
—44	France and Monaco
—45	Italy
—46	Spain

Class here, *without subdivision, Iberian Peninsula in general with adjacent islands*

—469	Portugal

Class here *Madeira, Azores*

—47	Union of Soviet Socialist Republics. Russia

Class here, *without subdivision, Eastern Europe in general. For USSR in Asia, see —57 and —58*

—48	Scandinavia

Class here, *without subdivision, Northern Europe in general*

—481	Norway
—485	Sweden
—489	Denmark
—489 7	Finland
—49	Other parts of Europe
—491	Iceland and the Faroes
—492	The Netherlands (Holland)

Class here, *without subdivision, the Low Countries in general and Benelux*

—493	Belgium and Luxembourg
—494	Switzerland
—495	Greece

For *Aegean Sea islands, see —499*

—496	Balkan peninsula
—497	Yugoslavia
—497 7	Bulgaria
—498	Romania
—499	Aegean Sea islands
—5	Asia

Class here, *without subdivision, general works on the Orient and the Far East*

—51	China and adjacent areas

Class here *Macao, Taiwan. For Korea, see —519*

—512 5	Hong Kong

—519	Korea
—52	Japan and adjacent areas
—53	Arabian peninsula and adjacent areas
	Bahrain, Kuwait, Oman, Peoples' Democratic Republic of Yemen, Qatar, Sinai peninsula. Saudi Arabia, United Arab Emirates, Yemen Arab Republic. Persian Gulf area in general
—54	India
	Class here the Indian sub-continent, India during British rule, the Indian state after British rule. For other jurisdictions, see —549
—541	Northeastern India
	Arunachal, Assam, Bihar, Manipur, Meghalaya, Mizoram, Nagaland, Orissa, Sikkim, Tripura, West Bengal
—542	Uttar Pradesh
—543	Madhya Pradesh
—544	Rajasthan
—545	The Panjab
—546	Jammu and Kashmir
—547	Western India
	Dadra, Daman, Diu, Goa, Gujarat, Maharashtra, Nagar Haveli
—548	Southern India
	Andaman and Nicobar Islands, Andhra Pradesh, Karnataka, Kerala, Lakshadweep, Tamil Nadu (Madras), Pondicherry
—549	Other jurisdictions
—549 1	Pakistan
—549 2	Bangladesh
—549 3	Sri Lanka
—549 5	The Maldives
—549 6	Nepal
—549 8	Bhutan
—55	Iran
—56	Middle East (Near East)
—561	Turkey
—564	Cyprus
—567	Iraq
—569	Countries of the Eastern Mediterranean
—569 1	Syria
—569 2	Lebanon
—569 4	Palestine. Israel
	For Jordan, see —5695

—569 5		Jordan
—57	Siberia	

Class here the USSR in Asia in general. For USSR, see
—47; Soviet republics in Central Asia, —58

—58	Central Asia	

Afghanistan, Soviet Republics in Central Asia

—59	Southeast Asia	
—591		Burma
—593		Thailand
—594		Laos
—595		Malaysia, Singapore, Brunei
—596		Cambodia (Khmer Republic, Kampuchea)
—597		Vietnam
—598		Indonesia
—599		Philippines
—6	Africa	
—611		Tunisia
—612		Libya
—62		Egypt

For Sinai Peninsula, see —53

—624		Sudan
—63		Ethiopia
—64		Northwest African coast and offshore islands
—642		Morocco
—648		Sahara (Western Sahara)

For Sahara Desert, see —66

—649		Canary Islands

Santa Cruz de Tenerife, Las Palmas (provinces of
Spain)

—65		Algeria
—66		West Africa and offshore islands

Benin, Burkina Faso, Cape Verde, Guinea-Bissau, Guinea
Republic, islands off the Gulf of Guinea, Ivory Coast,
Liberia, Mali, Mauritania, Niger, Senegal, Togo. Class
here Sahara desert

—664		Sierra Leone
—665		The Gambia
—667		Ghana
—669		Nigeria
—67		Central Africa and offshore islands

Angola, Burundi, Cameroon, Central African Republic,
Chad, Congo Republic, Djibouti, Equatorial Guinea,
Gabon, Rwanda, Somalia, Zaire. Class here Black Africa
in general, Africa south of the Sahara

33

—676	Uganda and Kenya
	Class here East Africa in general
—676 1	Uganda
—676 2	Kenya
—678	Tanzania
—679	Mozambique
—68	Southern Africa
	Class here, without subdivision, Southern Africa in general, the Republic of South Africa. For provinces of the Republic and for other jurisdictions, see 681–689
—681 1	Botswana
—681 3	Swaziland
—681 6	Lesotho
—682	Transvaal (Republic of South Africa)
—682 9	National States (Homelands)
	Bophuthatswana, Gazankulu, Lebowa, Venda, South Ndebele
—684	Natal (Republic of South Africa)
—684 9	National States (Homelands)
	KwaZulu
—685	Orange Free State (Republic of South Africa)
—685 9	National States (Homelands)
	Basotho-Qwaqwa
—687	Cape of Good Hope (Republic of South Africa)
—687 9	National States (Homelands)
	Transkei, Ciskei
—688	Namibia
	Including Walvis Bay exclave of Cape of Good Hope
—689	Zimbabwe, Zambia, Malawi
—689 1	Zimbabwe
—689 4	Zambia
—689 7	Malawi
—69	South Indian Ocean islands
—691	Malagasy Republic
—696	Seychelles
—698 2	Mauritius
—7	North and Central America
—71	Canada
—711	British Columbia
—712	Prairie Provinces
	Alberta, Manitoba, Saskatchewan. Class here Western Canada
—713	Ontario
	Class here Eastern Canada in general

—714	Quebec
—715	New Brunswick
	Class here Maritime Provinces in general
—716	Nova Scotia
—717	Prince Edward Island
—718	Newfoundland and adjacent territories. Labrador
—719	Northern Territories
	Class here Canadian Arctic
—72	Mexico
—728	Central America
—728 1	Guatemala
—728 2	Belize
—728 3	Honduras
—728 4	El Salvador
—728 5	Nicaragua
—728 6	Costa Rica
—728 7	Panama
—729	West Indies and Bermuda
—729 1	Cuba
—729 2	Jamaica and Cayman Islands
—729 3	Dominican Republic
—729 4	Haiti
—729 5	Puerto Rico
—729 6	Bahama Islands
—729 7	Leeward Islands
	Anguilla, Antigua, Guadeloupe, Montserrat, Saint Christopher-Nevis, Virgin Islands, Netherlands Islands
—729 8	Windward and other southern islands
	Aruba, Barbados, Bonaire, Carriacou, Curacao, Dominica, Grenada, Martinique, Saint Lucia, Saint Vincent and Grenadines, Trinidad and Tobago
—729 9	Bermuda
—73	United States
	For Hawaii, see —96
—74	Northeastern United States
	Connecticut, Maine, Massachusetts, New Hampshire, New Jersey, Pennsylvania, Rhode Island, Vermont
—747	New York
—75	Southeastern United States
	Delaware, Florida, Georgia, Maryland, North Carolina, South Carolina, Virginia, West Virginia
—753	District of Columbia (Washington, DC)

—76	South central United States, Gulf Coast states
	Alabama, Arkansas, Kentucky, Louisiana, Mississippi, Oklahoma, Tennessee
—764	Texas
—77	North central United States
	Illinois, Indiana, Iowa, Michigan, Minnesota, Missouri, Ohio, Wisconsin
—78	Western United States
	Colorado, Kansas, Montana, Nebraska, New Mexico, North Dakota, South Dakota, Wyoming
—79	Great Basin and Pacific Slope region Pacific Coast states
	Alaska, Arizona, Idaho, Nevada, Oregon, Utah, Washington
—794	California
—8	South America
	Class here, without subdivision, Spanish America, Latin America in general. For Mexico, Central America, and the West Indies, see —72
—81	Brazil
—82	Argentina
—83	Chile
—84	Bolivia
—85	Peru
—861	Colombia
—866	Ecuador
—87	Venezuela
—881	Guyana
—882	Guyane
—883	Surinam
—892	Paraguay
—895	Uruguay
—9	Other parts of the world and extraterrestrial worlds
—93	New Zealand and Melanesia
—931	New Zealand
—931 1	Outlying islands
—931 2	North Island
—931 27	Wellington (City)
—931 5	South Island and Stewart Island
—932	Melanesia
	Admiralty Islands, Bismarck Archipelago, Loyalty Islands, New Caledonia, New Hebrides (Vanuatu), Solomon Islands
—94	Australia
—941	Western Australia

—942   Central Australia
—943   Queensland
—944   New South Wales
—945   Victoria
—946   Tasmania
—947   Australian Capital Territory. Canberra
—948   Outlying islands
—95   New Guinea. Papua
—96   Other parts of the Pacific Polynesia
              Class here Hawaii (State of the U.S.A.)
—97   Atlantic Ocean islands
              For Azores, see —49
—971   Falklands and Bouvet
—973   Saint Helena and dependencies
—98   Arctic Islands and Antarctica
              For Antarctica specifically, see —989
—989   Antarctica
—99   Extraterrestrial worlds
              For space, see —19

Table 3   Subdivisions for Individual Literatures

This table is for use in conjunction with 810–890 (Literatures in individual languages) of Class 800. The numbers cannot be used alone or as prefixes. They can be added as suffixes to the base numbers of classes identified by an asterisk (*). The base numbers are the same as the class number unless otherwise indicated. A point is inserted between the third and fourth digits. Period numbers from Table 3P can be suffixed to —08–8. Note that permitted uses of Table 1 are indicated in this table. Table 3 and Table 3P may be used selectively or not at all as indicated for Table 1.

> Examples: English (Base number 82), poetry (—1 in this table), 821;
> Portuguese (Base and class number 869), poetry (—1 in this table), 869.1
>
> Anthologies of English literature (more than one form, more than one author), 82 + 08 = 820.8; history of English literature (more than one form, more than one author), 82 + 09 = 820.9
>
> Anthology of Elizabethan literature (more than one form and more than one author), 820.83 (for compatibility with unabridged edition, insert two zeros between 8 and 3, 820.8003). History of Elizabethan literature, 820.93 (for compatibility with unabridged edition, insert two zeros between 9 and 3, 820.9003)
>
> Elizabethan poetry (82 + 1 + 3), 821.3

—01–07   Standard subdivisions
       Notation from Table 1
—08   Collections
       More than one form, more than one author
—09   History, description, critical appraisal
       More than one form, more than one author
—1–8   Specific forms
       Class items by or about specific authors covering more than one form with the form most associated with the author (e.g., class Shakespeare in —2 drama rather than —1 poetry). Alternatively class collected works, biographies etc. at —8. For period divisions choose period in which author did most work. e.g., G. B. Shaw —91, early twentieth century.
—1   Poetry
—2   Drama
—3   Prose fiction (Novels, short stories)

—4	Essays

—4   Essays
Class here literary works. Class works on specific subjects with the subject

—5   Speeches
Note as at —4

—6   Letters
Note as at —4

—7   Satire and humour

—8   Miscellaneous writings
Examples: quotations, jokes, epigrams, experimental and non-formalized works. May be used for items by or about specific authors, covering more than one form; see note at —1–8

Table 3P   Period Subdivisions for Individual Literatures

For use as instructed at Table 3 (above). Subdivisions for other languages and other national outputs can be obtained from the schedules of the unabridged edition under each literature. See Introduction, paragraph 13.1.

Literature of the United States (Class 810)

—1   Colonial period, 1607–1776
—2   Post-Revolutionary period, 1776–1830
—3   Middle 19th century, 1830–1861
—4   Later 19th century, 1861–1900
—5   20th century
—52   Early, 1900–1945
—54   Later, 1945–

English literature

Use for English literature in general and for U.K. English literature. If other national outputs are to be distinguished and divided by period, extract period subdivisions from unabridged schedules (Classes 820 and 810)

—1   Early English period, 1066–1400
—2   Pre-Elizabethan period, 1400–1558
—3   Elizabethan period, 1558–1625
—4   Post-Elizabethan period, 1625–1702
—5   Queen Anne period, 1702–1745
—6   Later 18th century, 1745–1800

—7	Early 19th century, 1800–1837
—8	Victorian period, 1837–1900
—9	1900–
—91	20th century
—912	Early, 1900–1945
—914	Later, 1945–

French literature

Use for French literature in general and for French literature of France. If other national outputs are to be distinguished and divided by period, extract period subdivisions from unabridged schedules (Class 840)

—1	Early period to 1400
—2	15th century, 1400–1500
—3	16th century, 1500–1600
—4	Classical period 1600–1715
—5	18th century, 1715–1789
—6	Revolution and Empire, 1789–1815
—7	Constitutional monarchy, 1815–1848
—8	Later 19th century, 1848–1900
—9	1900
—91	20th century
—912	Early, 1900–1945
—914	Later, 1945–

Spanish literature

Use for Spanish literature in general and for Spanish literature of Spain. If other national outputs are to be distinguished and divided by period, extract period subdivisions from unabridged edition (Class 860)

—1	Early period to 1369
—2	Age of imitation, 1369–1516
—3	Golden Age, 1516–1700
—4	18th century, 1700–1800
—5	19th century, 1800–1900
—6	20th century
—62	Early, 1900–1945
—64	Later, 1945–

Table 4 Subdivisions for Individual Languages

This table is for use in conjunction with classes 420–490 (individual languages) of main class 400. The numbers cannot be used alone or as prefixes. They may be added as suffixes to the base number of classes indicated by an asterisk (*). The base number is the same as the class number unless otherwise indicated. A point is inserted between the third and fourth digits. Note that permitted uses of Table 1 are indicated in this table. Table 4 may be used selectively or not at all as described for Table 1:

> Examples: English (Base number 42), grammar (—5 in this table), 425; Portuguese (Base and class number 869), dictionaries (—3 in this table), 469.3

—01–09	Standard subdivisions *Notation from Table 1. For dictionaries, see —3, e.g. Portuguese dictionaries, 469.3 NOT 469.03*
—1	Written and spoken codes of the standard form of the language
—11	Notation *Writing systems, e.g. alphabets (visual and tactile), syllabaries, ideographic systems. Writing conventions, e.g., spelling, capitalization, punctuation, acronyms, abbreviations*
—15	Phonology of the standard form of the language *Sound system including phonetics and phonemics. Class here relationship of writing (e.g. spelling) to pronunciation*
—2	Etymology of the standard form of the language *Historical and grammatical derivation of words and morphemes: phonetic, graphic, semantic development. For writing in general, see —11; sound system in general —15; syntax in general, —5*
—3	Dictionaries of the standard form of the language *General dictionaries. Specialized dictionaries of special kinds of words and morphemes, e.g., acronyms, antonyms. Class bi-lingual dictionaries with language requiring emphasis, e.g., in a British school-library, class French-English dictionaries with French, i.e., with the foreign language. For polyglot dictionaries, see 413 (schedules)*
—5	Structural system (grammar) of the standard form of the language *Class here syntax and general descriptions of the language, including syntax, morphology, phonology. For morphology specifically, see —2; phonology specifically, —15. For prescriptive works, see —8*

41

—7   Nonstandard forms of the language. Language variety
           Regional and other dialects, slang, early forms, registers,
           other variety

—8   Usage (Prescriptive works)
           Guides to correct usage for native and foreign learners.
           Language "courses," travellers' guides

Summary of Schedules

SUMMARY OF SCHEDULES

A first-tier classification scheme for use in very small libraries

The following summary is intended for use in very small libraries, and might be especially appropriate for use in primary schools. It is compatible with the complete schedules which can be adopted in whole or in part as the library expands. The option to select a number or set of numbers from the complete schedules is open at any point, and in some cases a suggestion is made to that effect. This is done where the general heading might conceal a locally useful class or where no generally useful summarization is possible. For example, at 796 Athletic and outdoor sports and games, there is a reference to the complete schedules from which a locally favoured sport can be selected. Reference to the complete schedules may help to clarify the scope of a class, if this is not self-evident. For example, it might not be clear that indoor games and amusements at 793 includes puzzles, but this is made clear in the hierarchy of the complete schedules. Conversely, the correct placing of puzzles can be ascertained by consulting the alphabetical index, in which class numbers for the summary appear in parentheses if they differ from those in the complete schedules, e.g., Indoor games and amusements, 793, but Puzzles, Indoor amusements, 793.7 (793).

The summary can be extended by the selection of numbers from down the hierarchies in the complete schedules, *whether or not a suggestion is made to that effect*; and conversely can be abbreviated by the process of going up the hierarchies in the summary itself. For example, specific class numbers for labour, financial, land, and production economics need not be used, and all economics can be assigned to 330 without differentiation.

In some libraries it might be useful to colour code the classes for purposes of shelf arrangement. It is suggested that the colours should differentiate between the ten main classes, with a possible colour amalgamation between Classes 100 and 200. A colour code currently in use in some United Kingdom primary schools appears on p. 57.

CLASSES REPRESENTED IN BOLD TYPE IN THE COMPLETE SCHEDULES ARE THOSE WHICH APPEAR IN THIS SUMMARY.

000	Generalities. General knowledge
001	Knowledge
	Dissemination. Scholarship. Research. Spurious knowledge and frauds
004	Data processing. Computer science
010	Bibliography
	History and description of written and audio-visual records. History of the book and of printing
011	Bibliographies
	Bibliographies and library catalogues
020	Library and information science. Information retrieval. Descriptions of libraries. Guides to library use
028	Reading and the use of other information media
	Class here reading surveys. For reading in the educational curriculum, see 370
030	General encyclopaedias and information compendia
	Class subject encyclopaedias etc. with the subject
050	General serials and their indexes
	Periodicals, magazines, journals, school magazines. Class subject periodicals etc. with the subject
060	General organizations and museology
	Directories of organizations and museums. Museum organization. Class subject organizations with the subject
070	Journalism, publishing, newspapers
	For copies of journals etc., see 050

100	Philosophy
	For logic, see 160; ethics, 170
130	Paranormal phenomena and arts
	Occultism, witchcraft, fortunetelling, ghosts
150	Psychology
160	Logic
170	Ethics (Moral philosophy)
	Class here proper behaviour in general

200	Religion
220	The Bible
	The Holy Scriptures of Judaism and Christianity. Text and works about the Bible. Bible stories
221	Old Testament

225	New Testament
229	Apocrypha
229.8	Other inter-testamental works. Pseudepigrapha
230	Christianity
270	Historical and geographical treatment of Christianity

225   New Testament
229   Apocrypha
229.8   Other inter-testamental works. Pseudepigrapha
230   Christianity
270   Historical and geographical treatment of Christianity
        For specific denominations and sects if these are to be differentiated, see 280
280   Denominations and sects of the Christian Church
        Select as required class numbers from complete schedules
290   Other religions
        Select as required class numbers from complete schedules

300   The social sciences

301   Sociology. Anthropology
302   Social interaction
        Class here communication
303   Social processes
        Class here control, social change, conflict
304   Human ecology. Population. Movement of people
305   Social structure
        Social groups by age, sex, class, religion, language, race, occupation, condition
306   Culture
        Class here marriage, family, relationships of sexes
307   Communities
        Class here descriptions of the local community
310   Statistics
        General collections of statistics, census reports. Class statistics of a subject with the subject
320   Political science
326   Slavery and emancipation
330   Economics
331   Labour economics
332   Financial economics
333   Land economics
338   Production economics
340   Law
350   Public administration. Local and central government administration. The Civil service

355	Military art and science
	All branches of the armed services and supporting civilian services
360	Social problems and services
361	Social welfare. Social work
361.07	Study and teaching. School community projects. Awards for social work
362	Problems of and services to specific groups and types of persons
	Examples: physically handicapped, old people. Select as required class numbers from complete schedules
363	Other social problems and services
	Class here public works in general
363.1	Public safety
363.123	Water safety
	Examples: lifeboat services, swimming safety, water transport safety
363.125	Road safety
363.2	Police services
	For criminology, see 364
363.3	Disasters and the control of violence
363.4	Public morals
	Examples: control of drug traffic; gambling
363.5	Housing
363.6	Public utilities and related services
	Examples: water and power supply. For sanitation, see 363.7
363.7	Environmental problems and services. Environmental protection
	Class here sanitation and waste disposal
363.8	Food supply
364	Criminology and penology
366	Associations and clubs
	Examples: Freemasons, scouts, hereditary societies. Class an organization connected with a subject with the subject
370	Education
371.3	Methods of instruction and study
371.4	Guidance and counselling. Career guides
380	Commerce, communications, transportation
380.1	Commerce (Trade)
380.3	Communications
	For specific kinds, see 383–384

48

380.5	Transportation
	For specific kinds, see 385–388
383	Postal communications
384	Telecommunications
385	Railway transportation
386	Inland waterway and ferry transportation
387	Water, air, space transportation
387.7	Air and space transportation
388	Ground transportation
	For non-local railway transportation, see 385
388.4	Local transportation
390	Customs, etiquette, folklore
	Class in 390, without subdivision, works on customs and traditions, e.g., holidays, food, drink, marriage
395	Etiquette (Manners)
398	Folklore
398.2	Folk literature
	Class here traditional fairy tales, ghost stories, legends. Class anonymous classics and literature by identifiable authors in 800
398.5	Chapbooks, games, nursery rhymes, proverbs, puzzles, riddles

400 Language and language learning materials

420	English and Anglo-Saxon languages
429	Anglo-Saxon
430–490	Other languages
	Select as required class numbers from complete schedules

500 Pure sciences

510	Mathematics
511.3	Symbolic logic. Set theory
512	Algebra
513	Arithmetic
514	Topology
515	Analysis and calculus
516	Geometry and trigonometry
519	Probabilities and applied mathematics. Statistical mathematics
520	Astronomy and allied sciences
526.8	Map drawing and projections

527	Celestial navigation
529	Chronology. Time measurement and calendars
530	Physics
531	General mechanics
534	Sound and related vibrations
535	Optics and paraphotic phenomena. Light and colour
536	Heat
537	Electricity and electronics
538	Magnetism
539	Modern physics

539 Modern physics
Radiations. Molecular, atomic, nuclear physics

540 Chemistry and allied sciences

550 Earth sciences

551 Geology, meteorology, general hydrology

551.5 Meteorology
Study of the atmosphere

551.6 Climatology (Weather)

560 Palaeontology
Class here plant and animal fossils; prehistoric plant and animal life

570 Life sciences
For palaeontology, prehistoric life, see 560; botany, 580; zoology, 590

573 Physical anthropology
For social anthropology and anthropology in general, see 301

574 Biology

574.07 Study and teaching
Class here field study, nature trails, vivaria, wild life parks, conservation of plants and animals. For plants specifically (e.g., botanical gardens), see 580.7; animals specifically (e.g., zoos), see 590.7

574.1 Physiology, anatomy, morphology, pathology

574.5 Ecology

580 Botanical sciences

580.7 Study and teaching
See note at 574.07

581.9 Habitats and locations
Select as required class numbers from complete schedules

582–589	Genera and species
	Select as required class numbers from complete schedules
590	Zoological sciences
590.7	Study and teaching
	See note at 574.07
591	Zoology
591.04	Rare, vanishing, extinct species
592–599	Genera and species
	Select as required class numbers from complete schedules

600 Technology (Applied sciences)
Class works covering both pure and applied sciences in 500

604	General technologies
	See complete schedules
607	Study and teaching. Industrial research
608	Inventions and patents
610	Medical sciences
612	Human physiology and anatomy
613	General and personal hygiene. Healthy living
	Diet, exercise, rest, cleanliness
614	Public health and related topics
620	Engineering and allied operations
620.1	Engineering mechanics and materials
621	Applied physics. Mechanical engineering
621.1	Steam engineering
621.2	Hydraulic power technology
621.3	Electromagnetic and related branches of engineering
621.38	Electronic and communications engineering
621.39	Computer engineering
621.4	Heat engineering and prime movers
621.48	Nuclear engineering
621.5	Pneumatic, vacuum, low temperature engineering
621.8	Machine and tool engineering
622	Mining engineering and related operations. Quarrying
623	Military and nautical engineering
623.8	Nautical engineering. Naval architecture. Seamanship. Navigation
624	Civil engineering. Structural engineering
	For specific branches, see 625–629

625	Railway and road engineering
625.1	Railway and locomotive engineering
625.7	Road and traffic engineering
627	Hydraulic water engineering
	Engineering of waterways, harbours, ports, reservoirs, dams and other water-related structures. For hydraulic power technology, see 621.2; water supply, 628
628	Sanitary and municipal engineering
	Class here water supply, sewage treatment. For water engineering in general, see 627
629	Other branches of engineering
	Class here transport engineering in general
629.1	Aerospace engineering
	For astronautics, see 629.4
629.2	Automobile engineering
629.4	Astronautics
629.8	Automatic control engineering
	For computer engineering, see 621.39. Class applications of automatic control engineering with the subject, e.g., automatic control of machines 621.8
630	Agriculture and related topics
633	Field crops
634	Orchards, fruit, forestry
634.9	Forestry
635	Garden crops. Horticulture. Vegetable crops
635.9	Flowers and ornamental plants
636	Animal husbandry
	For specific animal groups, select as required class numbers from complete schedules
637	Dairy and related technologies
638	Insect culture
	Example: beekeeping
639	Non-domesticated animals and plants
	Hunting, fishing, trapping, gathering. Culture of non-domesticated animals (e.g., fish)
640	Home economics and family living. Domestic sciences
641	Food and drink (Nutrition)
641.5	Cookery
643	Housing and household equipment
646	Management of personal and family living. Sewing. Clothing

646.2	Sewing. Clothing
646.7	Management of personal and family living
	Class here personal appearance. For clothing, see
	646.2. Class here guides to behaviour and conduct
	of personal affairs, e.g., guides to retirement, married
	life, living alone
647	Management of public households. Hotel and catering management
648	Housekeeping
	Laundering, housecleaning, storage, moving
649	Child rearing and home nursing
650	Management and auxiliary services
651	Office services. Office management. Secretarial work and services
	Class here accountancy and bookkeeping
658	General management
	Class management of enterprises engaged in specific
	fields of activity with the subject, e.g., management of
	mines 622
658.8	Marketing. Salesmanship. Shops and shopping
659	Advertising and public relations
660	Chemical and related technologies
669	Metallurgy
	Class here general works on metals
670	Manufactures in specific materials
	Examples: metals, textiles. Select as required class numbers
	from complete schedules
680	Manufacture of products for specific purposes
	Examples: furnishings, printed books (printing
	technology). Select as required class numbers from
	complete schedules
690	Building and related technologies
	For design and construction in general, see 720; structural
	engineering, 624

700   The arts

For book arts, see 680; literary arts specifically, see 800

710	Civic and landscape art. Town and country planning
720	Architecture
	Class here design and construction in general. For building
	technology, see 690; structural engineering, 624

730	Sculpture
740	Drawing
745	Decorative and minor arts. Folk art
	Select as required class numbers from complete schedules.
	For interior decoration, see 747
746	Textile arts and handicrafts
747	Interior decoration
750	Painting
760	Graphic arts. Printmaking and prints
	For printing, see 680
770	Photography
780	Music
781	General principles and musical forms
781.6	Traditions of music
781.62	Folk music
781.64	Western popular music
	Class here jazz, rock 'n' roll
781.7	Sacred music
782	Vocal music
784	Instruments and instrumental ensembles and their music
	Select as required class numbers from complete schedules 784–788
790	Recreational and performing arts
	For music, see 780
790.1	Recreational activities in general. Hobbies in general
	General works and works on activities not otherwise specified, e.g., collecting; activities for specific kinds of persons, e.g., old people. Class a specific activity with the subject if this is specified, e.g., music as a hobby 780, athletics 796
791	Public performances
	Class here mass media as entertainment, circuses, pageants. For music, see 780; theatre, 792
792	Theatre
	For texts of plays, see 800
793	Indoor games and amusements
	Select as required class numbers from complete schedules 793–795
796	Athletics and outdoor sports and games
	Select as required class numbers from complete schedules 796–799

800	Literature (Belles-lettres)
	Class comprehensive works on the arts including literature in 700
810	American literature in English
	Divide like 820
820	English and Anglo-Saxon literatures
	Class Anglo-Saxon literature in 829
821	Poetry
822	Drama
823	Prose fiction (Novels and stories)
	If preferred, file in separate sequence using letter notation, e.g., "F" for fiction
824	Essays
825	Speeches
826	Letters
827	Satire and humour
	Class single works with the form in which they are written, e.g., humourous poetry 821
828	Miscellaneous writings
	Prose without specific form
829	Anglo-Saxon literature
830–890	Literature of other languages
	Select as required class numbers from complete schedules, using Table 3 if required, as instructed at 810–890

900	Geography, history and their auxiliaries
910	General geography and travel
	Not limited by location
910.3	Dictionaries, encyclopaedias, gazetteers
912	Atlases and maps in general
912.3–912.9	Atlases and maps of specific continents, countries, localities
	See complete schedules
913–919	Geography of and travel in specific continents, countries, localities, in the ancient and modern world, extraterrestrial worlds
	Select class numbers as required according to instructions in complete schedules 913–919
920	General biography. Genealogy. Names. Insignia
	If preferred, class biography of persons associated with a subject with the subject, e.g., biographies of scientists 500

929	Genealogy, names, insignia
930	History of the ancient world to ca. 499 A.D.
	Select as required class numbers from complete schedules
940–990	History of specific continents, countries, localities of the modern world
	Select as required class numbers for places and periods from the complete schedules, of which the following represents a selection:
940	Europe
941	The British Isles. United Kingdom. Great Britain
943	Germany
944	France
945	Italy
946	Spain
947	Union of Soviet Socialist Republics. Russia
	For USSR in Asia, see 950
948	Scandinavia
949	Other parts of Europe
950	Asia
960	Africa
970	North and Central America
971	Canada
973	United States
980	South America
990	Other parts of the world
993.1	New Zealand
994	Australia
995	Papua New Guinea

A SUGGESTED COLOUR CODE FOR PRIMARY SCHOOLS

000	Reference	Grey
100	Philosophy	⎫ Black
200	Scripture	⎭
300	Public services	⎫
	Transport	⎬ Orange
	Folk tales	⎭
400	Language	Brown
500	Sciences	⎫
550	Earth sciences	⎬ Yellow
551	Weather	⎭
560	Prehistoric animals	Yellow
570	Nature study in general	Green
580	Plants, trees, flowers	Green/red
590	Animals and birds	Green/gold
600	Technology	⎫
630	Agriculture, farming	⎬ Red
640	The home	
650–690	Industries	⎭
700	The arts	⎫
720	Architecture, castles, houses	⎬
750	Painting	Mauve
780	Music	
790	Recreation, games, sports, hobbies	⎭
800	Plays, poetry	Brown
900	General history	⎫
910	General geography	⎬ Blue
920	Biography	
930–990	History and geography of specific countries	⎭

Schedules

SCHEDULES

Classes represented in bold type in the complete schedules appear in the Summary of Schedules, pp. 45–56.

000   Generalities.   General knowledge

001   **Knowledge**
          History, description, critical appraisal of intellectual activity in general. Scholarship. Increase, modification, dissemination of information and understanding
001.4   Research
          Class research in a specific subject with the subject
001.9   Controversial knowledge
          Well-established phenomena not scientifically explained, e.g., fire walking; reported phenomena not fully verified, e.g., unidentified flying objects. Deceptions, hoaxes, errors. If preferred, class with subject, e.g., Piltdown man 573.3
003   Systems
          Class here systems theory, analysis, design

004   **Data processing.   Computer science**
          For engineering of computers, see 621.39. Class data processing and computer science applied to a specific subject with the subject, using "Standard Subdivisions" notation 028 from Table 1, e.g., data processing in banking 332.1028
004.1   General works on specific types of computers
          Examples: mainframe, minicomputers
004.16   Digital microcomputers
005   Computer programming, programs, data
          Class here data files, databases, data banks, computer security, computer graphics, artificial intelligence. For computer games, see 794
005.1   Programming and programming languages
005.3   Programs
          Collections of programs, systems of inter-related programs, individual programs having inter-disciplinary applications

010	**Bibliography**
	History, identification, description of written and audiovisual records. History of the book and of printing. For journalism, publishing and newspapers, see 070; printing and related technologies, 686; compilation of bibliographies, 025
011	**Bibliographies**
	Bibliographies and library catalogues
016	Subject bibliographies and catalogues
	Add 001–999 to base number 016, e.g., bibliography of astronomy, 016.52
020	**Library and information sciences**
	The science and art used in the identification, collection, organization, dissemination, and use of books, other printed and written records, audio-visual materials, information. For bibliography, see 010
025	Bibliographic analysis and control
	The compilation of bibliographies and catalogues. Library classification and information retrieval
027	Libraries
	Descriptions of and guides to libraries. Instructions on how to use libraries
028	**Reading and the use of other information media**
	Class here reading surveys. For reading in the educational curriculum, see 372
030	**General encyclopaedias and information compendia**
	Class subject encyclopaedias with the subject, using "Standard Subdivisions" notation 03 from Table 1, e.g., encyclopaedia of agriculture 630.3
050	**General serials and their indexes**
	Periodicals, magazines, journals. Class those on specific subjects with the subject, using "Standard Subdivisions" notation 05 from Table 1, e.g., science periodicals 505
060	**General organizations and museology**
	Class organizations devoted to a specific subject with the subject, using "Standard Subdivisions" notation 06 from Table 1, e.g., organizations devoted to medicine 610.6. Class here directories of general organizations

069   Museology (Museum science), museums and collections
Class here descriptions and directories. Class museums and collections devoted to a specific subject with the subject, using "Standard Subdivisions" notation 074 from Table 1, e.g., natural history museums 508.074

070   **Journalism, publishing, newspapers**
Journalism with respect to all media. For copies of periodicals etc., see 050

080   General collections
Miscellanies covering a wide range of topics. For general literary collections from more than one literature, see 808

090   Manuscripts and books rarities
If preferred, class with subject

100 Philosophy. Paranormal phenomena and arts. Psychology

Class general works on philosophy and on specific philosophical viewpoints (e.g., materialism, hedonism) in 100–109. However, class viewpoints with the subject if this is specified, e.g., materialist view of ethics 170. If preferred, works by and about individual philosophers and schools may be classed in 180–190, regardless of viewpoint. For logic, see 160; ethics, 170. For paranormal phenomena and arts, see 130; psychology, 150

109	History of philosophy
	If preferred, class works by and about individual philosophers and schools in 180–190
110	Metaphysics
111	Ontology
113	Cosmology
120	Epistemology. Causation. Humankind
121	Epistemology (Theory of knowledge)
122	Causation
	Chance, determinism
128	Humankind
	Philosophy of human life, the soul, life after death

130	**Paranormal phenomena and arts**
	Class phenomena of religious experience in 200
133	Parapsychology and occultism
133.1	Ghosts (Apparitions)
133.3	Divinatory arts
	Examples: fortunetelling, numerology, palmistry. For astrology, see 133.5; divinatory graphology, 137
133.4	Witchcraft. Demonology
133.5	Astrology
133.8	Psychic phenomena and extra-sensory perception
	Including clairvoyance, clairaudience. Class here psychic phenomena in general
133.9	Spiritualism
	The phenomena and systems of ideas connected with the belief in communication with discarnate spirits. For ghosts, see 133.1
137	Divinatory graphology
	Class here comprehensive works on graphology

150	**Psychology**

150 **Psychology**
Class psychology in relation to a subject with the subject, using "Standard Subdivision" notation 019 from Table 1, e.g., psychology of advertising 659.019. For social psychology, see 302; educational psychology, 370.1; clinical psychology, 616.89.

152 Physiological psychology
Senses, movement, emotions and feelings, physiological drives

153 Intelligence. Intellectual and conscious mental processes
153.9 Intelligence and aptitude tests and testing

154 Subconscious and altered states and processes (Depth psychology)
Class here the subconscious, daydreaming, sleep; states induced by drugs, hypnosis

155 Differential and genetic psychology
Psychology of individuals and classes of individuals as defined by age, sex, national or ethnic derivation, other factors. Environmental psychology

157 Abnormal psychology
For clinical psychology and psychiatry, see 616.89

158 Applied psychology
The use of psychology for the achievement of personal goals, e.g., excellence in leadership. See note at 150

160 **Logic**
For mathematical logic, see 511.3

170 **Ethics (Moral philosophy)**
Class here proper behaviour in general, ethical systems in general

172 Political ethics
Example: ethics of war

173 Ethics of family relationships
For ethics of sex and reproduction, see 176

174 Economic, professional, occupational ethics

175 Ethics of leisure and recreation
Class here sportsmanship, "fair play"; ethics of hunting and shooting, sports, gambling

176 Ethics of sex and reproduction
Class here ethics of prostitution, homosexuality, reproduction technology, pornography

177	Ethics of social relations
	Examples: discriminatory practices, gossip, hospitality, philanthropy
178	Ethics of consumption
	Class here abstinence, temperance; over-indulgence in the use of alcoholic beverages, food, narcotics
179	Other ethical norms
	Examples: treatment of animals, respect for life, capital punishment
180–190	Historical and geographical treatment of philosophy
	If preferred, class here development, description, critical appraisal, collected writings, biographical treatment of individual philosophers. Class comprehensive historical works in 100 and 109
180	Ancient, mediaeval, Oriental philosophy
181	Oriental philosphy
182	Ancient Greek philosophy
187	Ancient Roman philosophy
189	Mediaeval Western philosophy
190	Modern Western philosophy
191	United States and Canada
192	British Isles
193	Germany and Austria
194	France
195	Italy
196	Spain and Portugal
197	Russia and Finland
198	Scandinavia
199	Other countries

200   Religion

Class here religious mysticism, comparative religion

210   Natural religion and basic religious viewpoints
Examples: agnosticism, atheism, theism

215   Science and religion

220   **The Bible**
The Holy Scriptures of Judaism and Christianity. Class Christian Biblical theology in 230, Judaism in 296

220.3   Encyclopaedias and dictionaries

220.4   Original texts, early versions and translations

220.5   Modern versions
Example: King James Bible (Authorized version)

220.6   Interpretation and criticism (Exegesis)

220.7   Commentaries
Criticism and interpretation in textual order

220.9   Geography, history, persons of Bible lands in Bible times
Class here Bible stories retold

221–229   Specific parts of the Bible
Add to base numbers the numbers following 220 in 220.3–220.9:
commentaries on the Old Testament 221 + 7 = 221.7
modern texts of the New Testament 225 + 5 = 225.5
modern texts of the Gospels and Acts 226 + 5 = 226.5
commentaries on the Apocrypha 229 + 7 = 229.7

221   **Old Testament**

225   **New Testament**

226   Gospels and Acts of the Apostles

227   Epistles

228   Revelation (Apocalypse)

229   **Apocrypha**

229.8   **Other inter-testamental works. Pseudepigrapha**
Class here Dead Sea Scrolls

230–270   Specific elements of Christianity
Class here specific elements of specific denominations and sects, e.g., Roman Catholic religious orders 255. Class comprehensive works on Christianity and the Christian Church in 230

230   **Christianity in general.   Christian doctrinal theology**

231   Doctrines of God
Class here the Holy Trinity

232	Doctrines of Jesus Christ and his family. Christology
233	Humankind
	Examples: doctrines of original sin, freedom of choice, relationship to God
234	Salvation (Soteriology) and Grace
235	Spiritual beings
	Examples: saints, devils, angels. Class Mariology in 232
236	Eschatology
238	Creeds, confessions of faith, covenants, catechisms
	Examples: The Nicene Creed, the Westminster catechism. Class creeds and catechisms on a specific doctrine with the subject, e.g., attributes of God 231
240	Christian moral and devotional theology
241	Moral theology
	Sins, virtues, codes of conduct
242	Devotional literature
	Collections of prayers, meditations, hymns. For how to pray, see 248; public worship, 264; hymns with music, 782.27
246	Art in Christianity
	Religious significance and purpose. If preferred, class with particular art, e.g., religious architecture 726, sacred music 781.7. For hymns, see 242 and 782.27
247	Church furnishings
248	Christian experience, practice, life
	Examples: mysticism, conversion, prayer and meditation, witness bearing, stewardship, guides to Christian life for specific kinds of persons
248.092	Biographies and personal testimonies
250	The organization of the Christian Church at local level and Christian religious orders
253	Pastoral theology
	Duties and responsibilities of clergy and laity at local level
255	Religious congregations and orders
	Class here monks, nuns, religious brothers and sisters, monasticism
259	Parochial activities

260	Christian social and ecclesiastical theology

260   Christian social and ecclesiastical theology
Institutions, services, observances, work of Christianity and the Christian Church. For historical and geographical treatment, see 270; local churches and religious orders, 250; denominations and sects, 280

261   Social theology and inter-religious relations and attitudes
Attitude of Christianity to secular matters, e.g., war and peace, and to other religions. Class inter-denominationalism in 262

262   Church government, organization, nature (Ecclesiology)
Forms of Church organization, e.g., episcopal, presbyterian. Class here ecumenical movement. For papacy, see 282

263   Days, times, places of religious observance
Examples: Advent, Lent, feast and fast days, saints' days

264   Public worship
Services, ceremonies, rites (liturgy and ritual). For private devotion, see 248

265   Other rites, ceremonies, ordinances, sacraments
Examples: baptism, confirmation, matrimony

266   Missions and missionary societies
For missionary orders, see 255

267   Associations for religious work
Examples: Church Army, Young Women's Christian Association. For religious congregations and orders, see 255; missionary societies, 266

268   Religious training and instruction
Class here Sunday schools

269   Spiritual renewal
Examples: retreats, revivals

270   **Historical and geographical treatment of Christianity**
Class treatment of specific denominations and sects in 280; of specific doctrines and aspects with the subject, e.g., Immaculate Conception 232.

274–279   Treatment by continent, country, locality
Add "Areas" notation 4–9 from Table 2 to base number 27, e.g., the Christian Church in Asia 275

280	**Denominations and sects of the Christian Church**
	Class here general historical and geographical treatment of Christianity and the Christian Church and comprehensive works on specific denominations and sects and their local churches
281	Oriental and early churches
281.9	Eastern Orthodox churches
282	Roman Catholic Church
	Class here Catholicism in general, the papacy
283	Anglican churches
284	Protestant churches of continental origin and related bodies
	Examples: Lutheran, Moravian, Waldensian churches. Class here Protestantism in general
285	Presbyterian, American Reformed, Congregational churches
286	Baptist, Disciples of Christ, Adventist churches
287	Methodist churches
288	Unitarian churches
289	Other denominations and sects
289.3	Latter-Day Saints (Mormons)
289.5	Church of Christ, Scientist (Christian Science)
289.6	Society of Friends (Quakers)
289.9	Others
	Examples: Jehovah's Witnesses, Pentecostal Assemblies

290   **Other religions**

Classes identified by an asterisk (*) can be subdivided by the addition of the following numbers to the class number, e.g., rites of Judaism 296.3

1 Social theology and inter-religious relations
> *Attitudes to secular matters, e.g., war and peace, to other religions*

2 Doctrines

3 Public worship and other practices

4 Religious experience, life, practice
> *Examples: mysticism, conversion, prayer, meditation*

5 Moral theology
> *Sins, virtues, codes of conduct*

6 Leaders and organization

7 Activities inspired by religious motives
> *Examples: missions, religious training and instruction*

8 Sources

Class here holy scriptures and other writings.
Class the Bible (scriptures of Judaism and
Christianity) in 220

9 Sects and reform movements

292	*Classical (Greek and Roman) religion
293	*Germanic religions
294	*Religions of Indic origin
294.3	*Buddhism
294.4	*Jainism
294.5	*Hinduism
294.6	*Sikhism
295	*Zoroastrianism (Mazdaism, Parseeism)
296	*Judaism
297	*Islam
299	Other religions

300　The social sciences

Class here behavioural sciences, social studies. For psychology, see 150; language, 400. Class a specific application with the subject, e.g., sociology of World War II 940.53

300.1–300.9	Standard subdivisions
	Notation from Table 1

301　Sociology. Anthropology

For criminal anthropology, see 364; physical anthropology, 573

302–307　Specific topics in sociology

Unless otherwise instructed class works with two or more aspects with the aspect coming later in the schedules, e.g., mass media and population growth 304.6

302　　Social interaction.　Social psychology

302.2　　Communication

Class here mass media, sociolinguistics, the effect of media on specific groups. For language in general, see 400

302.3　　Group interaction

Examples: crowds, small groups, bureaucracies. Class here crowd psychology

302.5　　Individual in society

Class here deviation, alienation

303　　Social control, change, conflict

Class here socialization. Public opinion

303.4　　Causes and effects of social change. Social forecasts

Class here cultural exchange as a cause of social change. See note at 302–307

303.6　　Social conflict

Class here conflict resolution, pacifism, peace movements, sociology of war, peace studies

304　　Human ecology.　Population.　Movement of people

304.2　　Human ecology

For environmental problems, see 363.7; ecology in general, 574.5

304.5　　Sociobiology

Study of genetic bases of human behaviour

304.6　　Population

Growth, decline of populations. For movement of peoples, see 304.8; population programs and policies, 363.9

304.8	Movement of populations
	To areas larger than a community. For political
	aspects of immigration and emigration, see 325
304.83–304.89	Geographical treatment
	Add "Areas" notation 3–9 to base number 304.8
	preferring receiving area, e.g., movement to
	Australia 304.894

305   **Social structure (Social stratification)**
The roles and distinguishing features of social groups. Class here minorities and subcultures of specific groups, e.g., youth subculture 305.2. For subcultures in general, see 306.1

305.2	Age levels
	Class here youth culture, generation gap
305.3	Sexes
	Class here sexism, feminism
305.5	Social classes
	Class here social mobility
305.7	Language, ethnic, national groups
305.9	Other social groups

306   **Culture and institutions**
Class here ethnology, cultural and social anthropology

306.1	Subcultures
	For subcultures of specific social groups, see 305
306.3	Political and economic institutions
	Sociology of politics, economics, government
306.4	Cultural and religious institutions
	Sociology of knowledge, science, technology, art, religion. Cultural transmission. For dissemination of knowledge in general, see 001
306.7	Institutions relating to relationships of the sexes
	Class here courtship, prostitution, homosexuality. For marriage, see 306.8
306.8	Institutions pertaining to marriage and the family
	Class here types of marriage and family, kinship systems, e.g., nuclear, extended families, polygamy, tribes

307   **Communities**
Inter-acting populations in a relatively restricted area, e.g., cities and parts of cities. Class here general works on living conditions and people in particular areas, e.g., "our village," "our town"

307.7	Specific kinds of communities
307.72	Rural communities
	Class here village communities, rural sociology, country life
307.76	Urban and suburban communities
	Class here urban sociology, city (town) life

310 **Statistics**
General collections of statistics, census reports. Class statistics of a subject with the subject, e.g., birth and death statistics 304.6

320 **Political science**
Class here political theories, e.g, socialism, nationalism, apartheid

321 Forms of state and government
Examples: national, dependent, federal, feudal, monarchical, republican states

323 Internal relations of the state
Relationship of the state to organized groups, e.g., political parties, pressure groups; to individuals. Class here citizenship

323.4 Civil rights
For slavery, see 326

324 The political process
Class here voting, political parties, electoral systems

324.9 Geographical treatment of the political process
Add "Areas" notation 3–9 from Table 2 to base number 324.9, e.g., Europe 324.94, France 324.944. If preferred, class politics of the "home" country (i.e., that of the cataloguing agency) in 324 without subdivision

325 International migration
Immigration, emigration, colonization. For sociological aspects, see 304.8

325.09 Emigration from specific areas. Colonization by specific countries
Add "Areas" notation 4–9 from Table 2 to base number 325.09, e.g., colonization by Great Britain and emigration from the United Kingdom 325.0941. Prefer receiving area when this is specified, 325.4–325.9

325.4–325.9	Migration to, colonization of specific areas
	Add "Areas" notation 4–9 from Table 2 to base number 325, e.g., Australian immigrants to the United Kingdom 325.41, British colonization of Australia 325.94
326	**Slavery and emancipation**
	For human rights in general, see 323.4
327	International relations
	Including diplomacy, treaties, international aid and cooperation, espionage
328	Legislative bodies
330	**Economics**
	Class here comprehensive works on economics and commerce. For commerce specifically, see 380.1
330.01–330.09	Standard subdivisions
	Notation from Table 1
330.1	Systems and theories
	Examples: free enterprise, planned economies; schools of economic thought, e.g., Keynesianism
330.9	Economic situation and conditions
	Add "Areas" notation 3–9 from Table 2 to base numbers 330.9, e.g., an economic survey of the U.S.A. 330.973
331	**Labour economics**
331.1	Labour force and market
	Availability, composition, quality of labour force. Types of worker (e.g., female, juvenile, skilled, managerial, migrant)
331.8	Industrial relations
	Class here comprehenisve works on labour relations, bargaining disputes, conciliation. For personnel management, see 658.3
331.88	Trade (Labour) unions, workers' guilds, staff associations
332	**Financial economics**
	For public finance, see 336
332.1	Banks and banking
332.4	Mediums of exchange
	Money and barter. Class here monetary standards, international exchange, inflation and deflation, counterfeit money
332.6	Investment and investments
	Class here stock markets, investment guides. For banks and banking, see 332.1; insurance, 368

332.7	Credit
	Class here borrowing, mortgages, pawning, credit cards
333	**Land economics**
333.1	Ownership and control of land
	Class here real estate market, renting and leasing of property
333.7	Natural resources
	Class here comprehensive works on conservation, national parks
333.79	Subsurface resources
333.9	Other natural resources
	Examples: water, biological resources
336	Public finance
	Class here taxation. For tax law, see 343; national income, 339
337	International economics
338	**Production economics**
338.1	Agriculture
338.2	Extraction industries
338.4	Secondary industries and services
	For commerce, communications, transport, see 380
339	Macroeconomics and national income
340	**Law**
341	International law
341.2	The world community
341.22	The League of Nations
341.23	The United Nations
341.24	Regional associations and organizations
341.242	Europe
341.245	Western Hemisphere
341.246	Pacific
341.247	Asia
	Class here Arab League
341.249	Africa
	For Arab League, see 341.247
342–347	Other branches and aspects of the law
	Class works on laws of jurisdictions other than the "home" country in 349, e.g., in the United States, criminal law in general and criminal law of the United States 345; criminal law of Mexico 349.72

342	Constitutional law
	Class here comprehensive works on public law
343	Miscellaneous public law
	Examples: tax law, military law, regulation of trade
344	Social law
	Examples: labour law, social security, public health, educational law
345	Criminal law. Criminal procedure and courts
346	Private law
	Examples: bankruptcy; business, family law; inheritance, torts
347	Legal procedures and the courts
	For criminal procedure, see 345
349	Laws and law of individual states and nations
	Other than those of "home" country. Add "Areas" notation 4–9 to base number 349, e.g., law of United Kingdom 349.41

350	**Public administration. Military art and science**
	For military art and science specifically, see 355. Class in 350–354 executive branch of government, governmental administration, including that of government departments and government agencies, e.g., state-run industries. Class specific activities with the activity, e.g., railway administration 385
351	Central government in "home" country, and central governments in general
	National, state, provincial levels
352	Local government in "home" country, and local governments in general
	Examples: British county and borough levels
354	Public administration in countries other than the "home" country
	All levels
354.3–354.9	Specific areas
	Add "Areas" notation 3–9 to base number 354, e.g., Soviet Union and Moscow governments 354.47

355	**Military art and science**
	All branches of the armed services and supporting non-combatant services. Prefer specific branch, if this is specified, e.g., naval strategy 359. For military engineering, see 623

355.1	Military life and customs
	Examples: traditions, living conditions, uniforms, medals
355.3	Organization and personnel of military forces and supporting non-combatant services
	Class here historical units, e.g., yeomen of the guard, knights
355.4	Military operations
	Strategy, tactics, camouflage, transport, weaponry, equipments, installations, supplies
355.5	Training
356	Land forces and land warfare
	Class here armies in general
358	Air and space forces and air and space warfare
	Class here air forces in general
359	Naval forces and sea warfare
	Class here navies in general

360   **Social problems and services.   Associations**

361	**Social welfare**
361.07	**Study and teaching**
	Class here school community projects
361.3	Social work
361.6	Public action
	Class here the welfare state
361.7	Private and community action
	Coordination of action by government, individuals, charities, other non-governmental organizations

362	**Problems of and services to specific groups and types of persons**
	Prefer class coming earlier, e.g., deaf children 362.42
362.1	Illness and disability
	Class here comprehensive works on medical care
362.2	Mental and emotional illness, handicap
362.29	Addictions
362.3	Mental retardation
362.4	Physical handicaps
	For illness, see 362.1
362.41	Visual handicaps
	Class here deaf-blindness
362.42	Hearing handicaps
	For deaf-blindness, see 362.41
362.5	Poverty

362.6	Advanced age
362.7	Early age
	Children and young people
362.8	Other groups
	Examples: crime victims, families, women, specific ethnic groups, veterans (ex-service personnel)

363	**Other social problems and services**
	Class here public works in general. For transport, see 380
363.1	**Public safety**
363.11	Occupational and industrial hazards
363.12	Transport hazards
363.122	Railway transport
363.123	**Water transport**
	Class here water safety in general, including swimming safety, lifeboat services
363.124	Air and space transport
363.125	**Road safety**
363.13	Domestic hazards
363.14	Hazards in sports and recreation
363.15	Hazards in health care facilities
363.17	Hazardous materials
363.18	Hazardous machinery
363.19	Product hazards
	For food hazards, see 363.8
363.2	**Police services**
	For criminology, see 364
363.3	**Disasters. Control of violence**
363.37	Fire hazards
363.4	**Public morals**
	Examples: control of drug traffic, of gambling
363.5	**Housing**
363.6	**Public utilities and related services**
	For sanitation and waste collection and disposal, see 363.72
363.61	Water supply
363.62	Power supply
363.7	**Environmental problems and services. Environmental protection**
363.72	Sanitation. Waste collection and disposal
363.73	Environmental pollution
363.74	Noise
363.78	Pest control

363.8	Food supply
	Class here food safety and food inspection
363.9	Population problems
	Class here legal and quasi-legal control of population. For sociological aspects, see 304.6
364	**Criminology and penology**
	Class here general works on crime and punishment. For criminal law, see 345; police work, 363.2
364.9	Historical and geographical treatment of crime and punishment
	Add "Areas" notation 3–9 from Table 2 to base number 364.9, e.g., crime in the U.S.A. 364.973
365	Prisons and related institutions
	If preferred, class in 364
366	**Associations and clubs**
	Examples: freemasons, scouts, hereditary societies. Class an organization connected with an activity with the activity, e.g., music societies 780.6
368	Insurance
370	**Education**
	Class the study and teaching of a subject at an elementary level in 372; at higher levels with the subject, using "Standard Subdivisions" notation 07 from Table 1, e.g., the study of agriculture 630.7
370.1	Psychology, philosophy, and sociology of education
371	Generalities of education
	Prefer levels and kinds of education 372–379, e.g., teaching methods in primary education 372. For education and the state, see 379
371.1	Teachers and other personnel
371.3	**Methods of instruction and study**
371.32	Teaching materials
	Class teaching materials in relation to a specific subject with the subject. Class here works about teaching aids
371.4	**Guidance and counseling**
	Educational, vocational, personal counseling. Pastoral work. Class here career guides
371.9	Special education
	Education of students possessing characteristics which set them apart from the general population, e.g., blind, handicapped, gifted students

*Class here of all special edu
types of schools
for all pupils*

372	Primary education
	For special education, see 371.9
373	Secondary education
	For special education, see 371.9
374	Adult education
	Education outside the regular sequence of schools and courses. Non-vocational and recreational courses for adults. For special education, see 371.9
375	Curriculums
	Programmes of study
376	Single-sex education
	Class here general works on single-sex education, and general works on education of women. Prefer level, e.g., single-sex primary schools 372; higher education of women 378
378	Higher education
	For special education, see 371.9
379	Education and the state

380	**Commerce, communications, transportation**
380.1	**Commerce (Trade)**
	For economics, see 330; internal commerce, 381; international commerce, 382
380.3	**Communications**
	For specific kinds, see 383–384
380.5	**Transportation**
	For specific kinds, see 385–388
381	Internal commerce (Domestic trade)
382	International commerce (Foreign trade)
	Class here tariffs, trade agreements, balance of trade
383	**Postal communications**
384	**Telecommunications**
384.5	Radio and television
384.6	Telephone
385	**Railway transportation**
	For local transportation, see 388.4
386	**Inland waterway and ferry transportation**
386.3	River transportation
386.4	Canal transportation

387   Water, air, space transportation
             Class here comprehensive works on water
             transportation. For inland water and ferry
             transportation, see 386

387.1   Ports, terminals, lighthouses and other facilities
             For air transportation facilities, see 387.73

387.2   Craft
             For aircraft, see 387.73

387.5   Ocean transportation
             For craft, see 387.2

387.7   **Air transportation**
387.73   Aircraft and airports
387.8   Space transportation

388   **Ground transportation**
             For non-local railway transportation, see 385

388.1   Roads and highways
388.3   Vehicular transportation
             For local vehicular transportation, see 388.4

388.4   **Local transportation**
             Class here local road and rail transportation,
             including underground railways (subways); mass
             transit, urban transportation

390   **Customs. Etiquette. Folklore**
             Class etiquette specifically in 395; folklore specifically in
             398. For military customs, see 355.1

391   Costume and personal appearance
             Class here costume in general, fashion

392   Life cycle and domestic life
             Examples: Customs of birth, puberty, courtship,
             marriage, death, food, and drink

394   Other customs
             Examples: holidays, chivalry, diplomacy

395   **Etiquette (Good and bad manners)**
             Class here prescriptive works on how to behave

398   **Folklore**
             Class here theory, history of folklore. For works of and
             works about folk literature, see 398.2. However, class
             anonymous classics and literature by identifiable
             authors in 800. For religious mythology, see 200

398.2	Folk literature
	See note at 398
398.21	Fairy tales
398.22	Tales and lore of persons who lived or may have lived
	Examples: heroes, kings, magicians
398.23	Tales and lore of places and times
	Examples: Atlantis, golden age
398.24	Tales and lore of plants and animals
	Examples: dragons, phoenixes
398.25	Ghost stories
	For paranormal phenomena, see 133.1
398.26	Tales and lore of physical phenomena
	Examples: fire, water, weather
398.27	Tales and lore of everyday life
	Examples: food, love, marriage
398.5	**Chapbooks, games, nursery rhymes, puzzles, riddles, proverbs**

400   Language.   Linguistics

Class here comprehensive works on language and literature. For literature, see 800

401   Philosophy and theory
Class here universal languages. For artificial languages, see 499.9

409   Historical and geographical treatment
Add "Areas" notation —3–9 from Table 2 to base number 409, e.g., languages of Canada 409.71; of the British Isles 409.41

410   Linguistics
Class here linguistics in general, comparative linguistics, linguistics of Indo-European languages. For linguistics of other languages and groups of languages, see 420–490, for which Table 4 is available for subdivision

411   Notation
Alphabetic and non-alphabetic writing (including tactile and visual systems)

412   Etymology
Derivation and creation of words and morphemes: Phonetic, graphic, semantic development. For notation (writing), see 411; phonology, 414; grammar, 415

413   Polyglot dictionaries
For bilingual dictionaries, see —3 (Table 4) with the accompanying instruction. Class here lexicography

414   Phonology

415   Structural systems (Grammar)
Class here syntax and general works covering morphology, syntax, phonology. For morphology, see 412; phonology, 414

417   Dialects, dialectology, and language variety

419   Structured language other than spoken or written
Example: sign languages used by deaf persons

420–429   Specific languages and groups of languages
Each class identified by an asterisk (*) may be subdivided by adding "Subdivisions for individual languages" (Table 4) to the base number for the language. The base number is the same as the class number unless otherwise indicated. See Table 4 for examples

420   ***English and Anglo-Saxon languages**
Base number for English: 42. For Anglo-Saxon, see 429

429	**Anglo-Saxon**
430	*German
	Base number: 43. Class at 430 without subdivision Germanic languages in general and other languages and groups not otherwise specified. For English and Anglo-Saxon, see 420
439	Other Germanic languages
439.3	Netherlandish languages
439.31	*Dutch
439.36	*Afrikaans
439.7	*Swedish
439.8	*Danish
439.9	*Norwegian
440	*French
	Base number: 44. Class at 440 without subdivision Romance languages in general and specific Romance groups and languages not otherwise specified. For Italian, see 450; Spanish, 460; Portuguese, 469
450	*Italian
	Base number: 45
460	*Spanish
	Base number: 46
469	*Portuguese
470	*Latin
	Base number: 47. Class at 470 without subdivision Italic languages in general. For Romance languages, see 440
480	*Classical Greek
	Base number: 48. Class at 480 without subdivision Hellenic languages in general, classical (Greek and Latin) languages in general; specific Hellenic languages not otherwise specified. For Latin, see 470; Modern Greek, 489
489	*Modern Greek
490	Other languages
491	East Indo-European and Celtic languages
	For Indo-European languages in general, see 410
491.4	Indic languages
491.42	*Panjabi
491.43	*Hindi
491.44	*Urdu
491.45	*Bengali
491.46	*Assamese, *Bihari, *Marathi, *Oriya

491.47	*Gujarati and *Rajasthani
491.48	*Sinhalese
491.49	Other Indic languages
	Examples: Dard languages, e.g., Kashmiri; Romany
491.5	Iranian languages *Farsi
491.6	Celtic languages
491.62	*Irish Gaelic
491.63	*Scottish Gaelic
491.64	*Manx
491.66	*Welsh (Cymric)
491.67	*Cornish
491.68	*Breton
491.7	*Russian

Class here without subdivision East Slavic languages in general and specific East Slavic groups and languages not otherwise enumerated

| 491.8 | Slavic languages |

For East Slavic languages, see 491.7

| 491.85 | *Polish |
| 491.9 | Other Indo-European languages |

Examples: Latvian, Albanian

492	Afro-Asiatic (Hamito-Semitic) languages
492.4	*Hebrew
492.7	*Arabic
493	Hamitic and Chad languages

Examples: Coptic, Hausa

| 494 | Ural-Altaic, Paleosiberian, Dravidian languages |

Examples: Finnish, Hungarian, Tamil

| 495 | Sino-Tibetan and other languages of East and Southeast Asia |

For Malay languages, see 499.2

495.1	*Chinese languages
495.6	*Japanese
496	African languages

Examples: Ibo, Swahili, Yoruba, Zulu. For Afrikaans, see 439.36; Afro-Asiatic languages, 492; Hamitic and Chad languages, 493

497	North American native languages
498	South American native languages
499	Other languages

Class in 499 without subdivision specific groups and languages not otherwise enumerated, e.g., Australian languages, Polynesian languages, Basque

499.2   *Malay (Bahasa Malaysia)
             *Class here without subdivision Malay languages in
             general and specific groups and languages not
             otherwise enumerated, e.g., Tagalog, Balinese*
499.9   Artificial languages
             Examples: Esperanto, Interlingua

500   Pure sciences

Class here comprehensive works on pure and applied sciences. For applied sciences, see 600

508   Description and surveys of natural phenomena. Natural history
For descriptions of biological phenomena, see 574.9

510	**Mathematics**
511	Generalities
	Class here approximations, mathematical models
511.3	**Symbolic logic. Set theory**
512	**Algebra**
513	**Arithmetic**
514	**Topology**
515	**Analysis and calculus**
516	Geometry
519	**Probabilities and applied mathematics**
519.5	Statistical mathematics
520	**Astronomy and allied sciences**
521	Theoretical astronomy and celestial mechanics
522	Practical and spherical astronomy
	Class here observatories, telescopes
523	Descriptive astronomy
	Class here astrophysics
523.1	Universe (Cosmology)
	Origin, development, structure, destiny of the universe. Nebulas, galaxies, inter-stellar matter. For stars, see 523.8
523.2	Solar system
523.3	Moon
523.4	Planets
	For earth, see 525
523.5	Meteors, solar wind, zodiacal light
523.6	Comets
523.7	Sun
523.8	Stars
	For sun, see 523.7
525	Earth
	Dimensions, properties, orbits, motions, seasons and zones, tides

526	Mathematical geography. Geodesy
526.8	**Map drawing and projections**
	For map reading, see 912
526.9	Surveying
	Class here geodetic surveying

| 527 | **Celestial navigation** |
| | *Determination of geographic position and direction. Class specific application with the subject, e.g., in seamanship 623.8* |

| 529 | **Chronology** |
| | *Class here calendars, finding and measuring time. For clock and watch design and manufacture, see 681* |

| 530 | Physics |
| | *Class here mathematical physics, relativity, states of matter, quantum theory* |

531	**General mechanics**
	Class here mechanics of solids
532	Mechanics of fluids
533	Mechanics of gases

| 534 | **Sound and related vibrations** |

535	**Optics and paraphotic phenomena**
	Class optical instruments for specific purposes with the subject, e.g., telescopes 522, microscopes 578
535.6	Colour
535.8	Spectroscopy and light not visible to the eye

| 536 | **Heat** |
| | *Class here heat transfer, temperature, thermodynamics* |

537	**Electricity and electronics**
537.2	Electrostatics
537.5	Electronics
537.6	Electric currents and thermoelectricity
	Class here semi- and superconductivity

| 538 | **Magnetism** |

539	**Modern physics**
539.2	Radiations
539.6	Molecular physics
539.7	Atomic and nuclear physics
	Class here nuclear reactions, X-, gamma, and cosmic rays

540	Chemistry and allied sciences
541	Physical and theoretical chemistry
542	Chemical laboratories, apparatus, equipment, procedures
543	Analytical chemistry
546	Inorganic chemistry
547	Organic chemistry
548	Crystallography
549	Mineralogy

For crystallography, see 548; geology, 553

| 550 | **Earth sciences** |

Class here non-astronomical aspects of other worlds

| 551 | **Geology, meteorology, general hydrology** |

For geodesy, see 526; physical geography, 910.02

| 551.1 | Gross structures and properties of the earth and other worlds |
| 551.2 | Plutonic phenomena |

Examples: volcanoes, earthquakes, geysers. Class here seismology, plate tectonics

| 551.3 | Surface phenomena |

Examples: erosion, sedimentation, weathering action of ice, wind. Class here glaciology, comprehensive works on ice

| 551.4 | Land forms and water |

Class here oceanography, hydrology. For effect of ice and water on land, see 551.3

| 551.5 | **Meteorology** |

Properties and phenomena of the atmosphere

| 551.6 | **Climatology (Weather)** |
| 551.7 | Historical geology |

Class here stratigraphy

| 551.8 | Structural geology and petrology |
| 553 | Economic geology |

Distribution and deposit of geological materials of value to mankind

| 554–559 | Regional geology |

Add "Areas" notation 4–9 from Table 2 to base number 55, e.g., the geology of North America 557.3

| 560 | **Paleontology** |

Class here general works on prehistoric life

| 561 | Paleobotany |
| 562 | Paleozoology |

567	Cold-blooded vertebrates
	Class here dinosaurs
568	Birds
569	Mammals
570	**Life sciences**
	For botany, see 580; zoology, 590
572	Human races
	For social aspects, see 300
572.9	Geographical treatment
	Add "Areas" notation 1–9 from Table 2 to base number 572.9, e.g., races of Europe, 572.94; the Mediterranean region 572.9182
573	**Physical anthropology**
	For anthropology in general, social anthropology, see 301
573.3	Prehistoric man
574	**Biology**
	For botany, see 580; zoology, 590
574.07	**Study and teaching**
	Class here field study, nature trails, vivaria, wild life parks, conservation. For plants specifically, see 580.7; animals specifically, 590.7
574.1	**Physiology, anatomy, morphology, pathology**
574.19	Biophysics. Biochemistry
574.5	**Ecology**
	For human ecology, see 304.2
574.6	Economic biology
	Organisms beneficial or deleterious to man's interests
574.8	Tissue, cellular, molecular biology
574.9	Geographical treatment
574.909	Habitats
	Add "Areas" notation 1 from Table 2 to base number 574.909, omitting initial "1", e.g., 154 deserts = 54, 574.90954 desert biology. For hydrographic biology, see 574.92
574.92	Hydrographic biology. Marine biology
574.96–574.99	Continents, countries, localities
	Add "Areas" notation 4–9 from Table 2 to base number 574.9, e.g., plants and animals of Africa 574.96
575	Organic evolution and genetics

| 576 | Microbiology |
| 578 | Microscopy in biology and other life sciences |

580   **Botanical sciences**

For paleobotany, see 561. Prefer classes coming later in the schedules, e.g., ferns of Brazil 587, not 581.981

580.7   **Study and teaching**

Class here field study, nature trails, plant collections, wild life parks, plant conservation. For plants and animals in general, see 574.07

581	Botany
581.1	Physiology, anatomy, morphology, pathology
581.3	Reproduction, development, maturation
581.5	Ecology
581.6	Economic botany

Plants beneficial or deleterious to man's interests. Class here botanical aspects of weeds, plants as pests, food plants. For general works on these subjects, see 630 Agriculture.

| 581.8 | Tissue, cellular, molecular botany |

581.9   **Geographical treatment**

Habitats and locations. Add "Areas" notation 1–9 from Table 2 to base number 581.9, e.g., desert plants 581.9154, plants of Scotland 581.9411

| 582 | Spermatophyta (Seed-bearing plants) |

Class here shrubs, woody plants

| 582.16 | Trees |

    Class here dendrology

| 583 | Dictotyledons |

    Examples: cacti, heather, roses

| 584 | Monocotyledons |

    Examples: palms, rice, orchids

| 585 | Gymnosperms |

    Examples: conifers, yews

| 586 | Cryptogamia (Seedless plants) |
| 587 | Pteridophyta |

    Example: ferns

| 588 | Bryophyta |

    Example: mosses

| 589 | Thallophyta |

    Examples: fungi, algae

| 589.9 | Schizophyta (Fission plants) |

    Class here bacteria, bacteriology

590	**Zoological sciences**
	For paleozoology, see 562. Prefer classes coming later in the schedules, e.g., physiology of insects 595.7, not 591.1
590.7	**Study and teaching**
	Class here field study, nature trails, zoos, nature reserves, animal collections, animal conservation
591	**Zoology**
591.04	**Rare, vanishing, extinct species**
591.1	Physiology, anatomy, morphology, pathology
591.3	Reproduction, development, maturation
	Class here the young of animals, e.g., books about "baby animals"
591.5	Ecology, adaptation, behaviour, psychology
591.6	Economic zoology
	Animals, beneficial or deleterious to man's interests. Class here zoological aspects of working animals, food animals, pet animals, animals as pests. For general works on these subjects, see 636 animal husbandry.
591.8	Tissue, cellular, molecular zoology
591.9	Geographical treatment
	Habitats and locations. Add "Areas" notation 1–9 from Table 2 to base number 591.9, e.g., desert animals 591.9154; animals of Scotland 591.9411
592	Invertebrates
593	Protozoa and other simple animals
	Examples; sponges, jellyfish
594	Mollusks and related animals
	Examples: clams, oysters, slugs, snails, octopuses
595	Other invertebrates
	Examples: leeches, scorpions, spiders, ticks, worms
595.7	Insects
	Examples: ants, beetles, butterflies, lice
596	Vertebrates. Chordates
597	Cold-blooded vertebrates
597.3	Fishes
	Class here sharks, ganoids
597.6	Amphibians
	Examples: frogs, salamanders, toads
597.9	Reptiles
	Examples: turtles, lizards, snakes, crocodiles

598	Birds. Ornithology
598.04	Rare, vanishing, extinct species
598.07	Study and teaching

Class here field study, nature trails, aviaries, conservation. For plants and animals in general, see 574.07. Class here bird watching, bird banding

598.09	Geographical treatment

Habitats and locations. Add "Areas" notation 1, 4–9 from Table 2 to base number 598.09, e.g., tropical birds 598.0913, birds of Scotland 598.9411

598.3	Water birds

Examples: cranes, gulls, sandpipers

598.5	Ostriches and related birds
598.6	Galliformes and Columbiformes

Examples: turkeys, pigeons, doves

598.7	Psittaciformes and related orders

Examples: parrots, toucans, roadrunners, cuckoos

598.8	Passeriformes (Perching birds), Coraciiformes, Apodiformes

Examples: larks, sparrows, cardinals, kingfishers, swifts

598.9	Falconiformes (Birds of prey), Strigiformes, Caprimulgiformes

Examples: vultures, owls, frogmouths

599	Mammals

Class here warm-blooded vertebrates in general. For birds, see 598

599.04	Rare, vanishing, extinct species
599.09	Geographical treatment

Habitats and location. Add "Areas" notation 1–9 from Table 2 to base number 599.09, e.g., mammals of cold regions 599.0911; urban habitats 599.091732; European mammals 599.094

599.1	Monotremata

Examples: kangaroos, wombats

599.3	Unguiculata

Examples: armadillos, rabbits, rodents, squirrels, moles

599.5	Cetacea and Sirenia

Examples: dolphins, porpoises, whales

599.6	Paenungulata
	Examples: elephants, hyraxes. For sirenia, see 599.5
599.7	Ferungulata and Tubulidentata
	For Paenungulata, see 599.6
599.72	Odd-toed ungulates
	Examples: rhinoceroses, tapirs
599.725	Equidae (Horses, asses, zebras)
599.73	Even-toed ungulates
	Examples: bison, camels, deer, giraffes, pigs, sheep
599.74	Carnivora
	Examples: bears, cats, dogs, otters, racoons, seals, walruses
599.8	Primates
	Examples: apes, baboons, monkeys. Class here Hominoidea in general. For hominidae, see 599.9
599.9	Hominidae (Humankind and forebears)
	For physical anthropology, see 573; human anatomy and physiology, 611–612

600   Technology (Applied sciences)

Class comprehensive works on pure and applied sciences in 500, on society and technology in 300

604	**General technologies**
604.2	Technical drawing
604.6	Waste technology
604.7	Hazardous materials technology
607	**Studying and teaching**
	Class here industrial research
608	**Inventions and patents**
610	**Medical sciences**
610.7	Studying and teaching
610.73	Nursing and other activities ancillary to medicine
611	Human anatomy, cytology, tissue biology
	For comprehensive works on human anatomy and physiology, see 612

612	**Human physiology**
	Class here comprehensive works on human anatomy and physiology
612.014	Biophysics
612.015	Biochemistry
612.1	Blood and circulation
612.2	Respiration
612.3	Nutrition
612.4	Secretion, excretion, bone marrow
612.6	Reproduction, development, maturation
	Class here comprehensive works on "growing up." For birth control, see 613.9.
612.7	Motor function and integument
612.8	Nervous and sensory functions
612.82	Brain and spinal cord
612.84	Eyes and vision
612.85	Ears and hearing
612.86	Nasal organs and smelling
612.87	Taste organs and tasting
612.88	Sensory organs for touch, movement, autonomic systems

613	**General and personal hygiene, mental health**
	Class here works on "healthy living"
613.2	Nutrition. Dietetics
613.4	Personal cleanliness

613.6	Personal safety
613.7	Physical fitness
	Class here works on exercise, rest, sleep. For nutrition, see 613.2
613.8	Addictions
	Examples: alcohol, drugs, tobacco
613.9	Sex health and techniques
	Class here birth control
614	**Public health and related topics**
614.1	Forensic medicine
614.4	Incidence, distribution, control of disease
615	Therapeutics and pharmacology
615.1	Pharmacology. Drugs
	For drug therapy, see 615.5; toxicology, 615.9
615.5	Therapeutic systems
	Examples: allopathy, homeopathy, naturopathy, drug therapy. Class here "alternative medicine" in general
615.8	Special therapies
	Examples: dance therapy, flower therapy. Class here folk medicine in general. For drug therapy, see 615.5
615.9	Toxicology (Poisons and poisoning)
616	Diseases and injuries
	Causes, effects, diagnosis, prognosis, treatment, prevention. For surgery, see 617; wounds, 617.1; diseases of women, children, the aged, 618
616.02	First aid
616–616.8	Diseases by system affected
	For regional medicine, see 617
616.1	Cardio-vascular system
616.2	Respiratory system
616.3	Digestive system
616.4	Blood-forming, lymphatic, glandular, endocrine systems
616.5	Skin, hair, nails
616.6	Genito-urinary system
	For gynaecology, see 618.1
616.7	Musculo-skeletal system
	Muscle and bones
616.8	Nervous system. The mind
616.89	Psychiatric disorders

616.9	Other diseases
	Not defined by system or region affected. Examples: communicable diseases, cancer. For diseases of women, children, the aged, see 618
617	Surgery and related topics
	Class here regional medicine, traumatology, anaesthesia
617.1	Wounds
617.6	Dentistry
617.7	Ophthalmology
	Eye diseases and injuries
617.8	Otology and audiology
	Hearing diseases and injuries
618	Other branches of medicine
618.1	Gynaecology and obstetrics
618.92	Paediatrics
618.97	Geriatrics
619	Experimental medicine
	The use of animals to study human diseases
620	**Engineering and allied operations**
620.01–620.09	Standard subdivisions
	Notation from Table 1
620.1	**Engineering mechanics and materials**
620.2	Sound and related vibrations
	Applied acoustics, ultrasonics, subsonics, noise control
620.3	Mechanical vibration
620.7	Systems engineering
620.8	Environmental engineering
	Engineering for human comfort, convenience, health, safety. Ergonomics
621	**Applied physics**
	Mechanical, electrical, electronic, electromagnetic, heat, light, nuclear engineering
621.1	**Steam engineering**
621.2	**Hydraulic-power technology**
	Examples: water wheels, hydraulic pumps, rams
621.3	**Electromagnetic and related branches of engineering**
	Generation, modification, storage, transmission of electric power
621.32	Lighting
621.34	Magnetic engineering
621.36	Optical and paraphotic engineering
	Examples: laser technology, holography

621.37	Electrical testing and measurement

621.37   Electrical testing and measurement
Class testing and measurement of specific apparatus, part or function with the subject, using "Standard subdivision" notation 028 from Table 1, e.g., testing lighting 621.32028

621.38   **Electronic and communications engineering**

621.381   Electronics engineering
For computer engineering, see 621.39

621.384   Radio engineering

621.388   Television engineering

621.39   **Computer engineering**

621.4   **Heat engineering and prime movers. Solar engineering**

621.48   **Nuclear engineering**

621.5   **Pneumatic, vacuum, low temperature engineering**
Examples: compressors, pumps, refrigerators, fans

621.8   **Machine engineering**
Theory, design, construction, installation of machinery, mechanical systems, related mechanisms. Examples: valves, lathes, cranes

621.9   Hand tools

622   **Mining engineering and related operations**
Prospecting for and extraction of minerals and other deposits from surface, subsurface, and underwater locations. Class here quarrying

623   **Military and nautical engineering**
For comprehensive works on military science, see 355

623.4   Weaponry (Ordnance)

623.6   Transportation and other military operations
For nautical craft, see 623.8

623.8   **Naval (Nautical) engineering**
Design, construction, maintenance and repair of boats and ships. Class here seamanship, navigation, rescue operations

624   **Civil engineering**
For specific branches, see 625–629

624.1   Foundations and structures. Structural engineering
For building technology, see 690

624.2   Bridges

625   **Railway and road engineering**
For bridges, see 624.2

625.1	**Railways**
625.2	Permanent way
	Class here track, track accessories (e.g., signals), yards, stations, other non-mobile equipment
625.7	**Road and traffic engineering**
	Class here traffic control equipment, parking facilities, service stations
627	**Hydraulic (Water) engineering**
	Engineering of waterways, harbours, parks, reservoirs, dams, other water-related structures
628	**Sanitary and municipal engineering**
	Class here water supply, sewage treatment, fire safety. For comprehensive works on water engineering, see 627; disposal of radioactive waste, 621.48
629	**Other branches of engineering**
	Class here transport engineering in general. For railway road and traffic engineering, see 625
629.1	**Aerospace engineering**
	Class here aeronautical engineering. For astronautics, see 629.4
629.2	**Automobile engineering**
	Engineering of automobiles, motorcycles, and related vehicles
629.4	**Astronautics**
629.8	**Automatic control engineering**
	For computer engineering, see 621.39. Class application of automatic control engineering with the subject, e.g., numerical control of machine tools 621.8
630	**Agriculture and related technologies**
631	Agricultural principles and techniques
	Class specific applications with the subject, e.g., harvesting of wheat 633
631.2	Agricultural structures, tools, machinery equipment
	Examples: barns, silos, harvesters
631.4	Soil and soil conservation. Soil science
631.5	Cultivation and harvesting
632	Plant injuries, diseases, pests
	Class injuries, diseases, pests of specific crops in 633–635
633	**Field crops**
	Large scale production of crops other than fruit and vegetables

634	Orchards, fruit, forestry
634.9	Forestry
635	Garden crops. Horticulture. Vegetable culture
635.9	Flowers and ornamental plants
636	**Animal husbandry**

Production, maintenance, training of livestock and domestic animals

636.08	Generalities of animals

Examples: breeding, transport, consumption. Class specific applications with the animal, e.g., breeding of dogs 636.7

636.088	Animals as pets

Class here general works on animals as pets. For zoological aspects, see 591.6

636.089	Veterinary medicine
636.1	Horses and other equines

Examples: donkeys, mules, zebras

636.2	Ruminants, bovines, cattle

Examples: beef cattle, bison, camels

636.3	Goats, sheep and related animals
636.4	Pigs
636.5	Poultry

For egg production, see 637

636.6	Birds other than poultry

Examples: gamebirds, ornamental birds

636.7	Dogs and related animals
636.8	Cats and related animals
636.9	Other warm-blooded animals

Examples: kangaroos, minks

637	**Dairy and related technologies**

Production, processing, and marketing of milk, eggs, and products derived from them

638	**Insect culture**

Culture of bees, silkworms, and other insects. Production of honey and beeswax

639	**Non-domesticated animals and plants**

Hunting, fishing, trapping, culture. Class animals and plants not enumerated here in 636, e.g., hunting of tigers 636.8. For sporting aspects, see 799; insect culture, 638

639.1	Hunting and trapping

639.2	Commercial fishing, whaling, sealing
639.3	Culture of cold-blooded vertebrates
	Class here fish farming
639.4	Culture of mollusks and crustaceans
	Examples: oysters, clams, lobsters
639.9	Conservation of biological resources
	Technologies devised to maintain, increase, reduce populations of animals and plants in their natural habitats
640	**Home economics and family living (Domestic science)**
641	**Food and drink. Nutrition**
	For medical aspects of nutrition, see 613.2
641.2	Drink
641.3	Food and foodstuffs
	For alcoholic and non-alcoholic drinks, see 641.2
641.4	Preservation and storage
641.5	**Cooking**
	Preparation of food with or without heat (other than for preservation and storage). Class here recipes
641.59	Cooking and recipes of specific locales
	Add "Areas" notation 4–9 from Table 2 to base number 641.59, e.g., Chinese cooking 641.5951
641.6	Cooking processes. Cooking with specific materials
	Examples: pickling, boiling, vegetarian recipes
642	Meals and table service
	Meal and menu planning; place settings, table furnishings, meal etiquette
643	**Housing and household equipment**
643.1	Choosing and acquiring housing
643.3	Decorating, equipping the residence
	For design and decorative treatment, see 747
644	Household utilities
	Examples: heating, lighting, ventilating, sanitation, water supply
646	**Management of personal and family living. Sewing. Clothing**
646.2	**Sewing**
	For clothing construction, see 646.4
646.3	Clothing
	Description, selection, acquisition, of clothing for utility, economy, appearance. Care of clothing

646.4	Clothing construction
	Class here home dressmaking
646.7	**Management of personal and family living**
	Class here general guides to conduct of personal affairs, e.g., to retirement living, behaviour in adolescence
646.71	Physical appearance
	For clothing, see 646.3
646.76	Social behaviour
	Examples: choice of mate, dating behaviour
646.77	Family living
	Class here guides to harmonious family relationships. For child rearing, see 649.1
647	**Management of public households. Hotel and catering management**
648	**Housekeeping**
	Laundering, housecleaning, storage, moving
649	**Child rearing and home nursing**
649.1	Child rearing
649.8	Home nursing
650	**Management and auxiliary services**
651	**Office services. Office management**
651.2	Equipment and supplies
651.3	Secretarial services
651.5	Records management
	Class here microreproduction and computerization of records, files and filing
651.7	Communications. Creation and transmission of records
652	Writing, typewriting, duplication, cryptography
	For shorthand, see 653
653	Shorthand
657	Accountancy and bookkeeping
658	**General management**
	Class the management of enterprises engaged in specific fields of activity with the subject, using "Standard subdivisions" notation 06 from Table 1, e.g., management of mines 622.06. For public administration, see 350

658.1	Organization and finance
658.11	Types of organization
	Examples: partnerships, limited companies
658.15	Financial management
658.2	Plant management
	Buildings, grounds, equipment, facilities
658.3	Personnel management
	For labour economics, see 331
658.5	Production management
	Class here work study, quality control, procurement, materials management
658.8	**Marketing**
	Class here salesmanship, shops and shopping, wholesale and retail distribution. For advertising and public relations, see 659
659	**Advertising and public relations**
660	**Chemical and related technologies**
	For pharmaceutical chemistry, see 615.1; elastomer and elastomer products, 678
660.2	Chemical engineering
661	Technology of industrial chemicals
	Large scale production of chemicals used as raw materials or reagents in the manufacuture of other products. Examples: acids, alkalis, sulfates, nitrates, coal tar
662	Technology of explosives, fuels, and related products
	For coal mining and petroleum exploration, see 622; industrial oils and gases 665
663	Technology of drinks
	For food technology in general, see 664
664	Food technology
	Industrial manufacture and packaging of edible products for human and animal consumption. For technology of drinks, see 663; dairy and related technologies, 637
665	Technology of industrial oils, fats, waxes, gases
	Examples: animal fats and oils, petroleum technology. For petroleum exploration, see 622
666	Ceramics and related technologies
	Examples: glass, pottery, concrete
667	Cleaning, colouring, coating, and related technologies
	Examples: bleaching, dyeing, painting

668	Technology of other organic products
	Examples: soaps, adhesives, plastics, perfumes,
	cosmetics, fertilizers, pesticides, polymers
669	**Metallurgy**
	Class here general works on metals
670	**Manufactures in specific materials**
	Planning, design, fabrication of products. Class here
	comprehensive works on manufacturing. Class arts in 700,
	manufactures based on chemical technologies in 660,
	engineering products other than those listed in 660–680 in 620
671	Metals manufacture
	Foundry practice, metal forming, cutting, joining,
	finishing; primary products
672	Ferrous metals
673	Non-ferrous metals
674	Lumber, cork, and wood-using technologies
	For carpentry, see 694
675	Leather and fur technologies
	For leather and fur goods, see 685
676	Pulp and paper technology
677	Textiles technology
	Class textiles arts and handicrafts in 746
678	Elastomers and elastomer products
	Rubber, latex, elastoplastics
679	Other products of various specific materials
	Examples: ivory, feathers, brooms, tobacco
680	**Manufacture of products for specific purposes**
681	Precision instruments and related devices
	Examples: clocks, microscopes, musical instruments.
	Class specific applications with the subject, e.g., aircraft
	instruments 629.1
682	Blacksmithing (Small forge work)
683	Hardware and household appliances
	Examples: pots, pans, electric equipment
683.3	Locksmithing
683.4	Small firearms. Gunsmithing
684	Furnishings
	Class here woodworking
684.1	Furniture
684.3	Fabric materials and goods

685	Leather and fur technology and goods, and related manufactures
	Class here camping equipment, saddlery, shoes, gloves; luggage irrespective of materials
686	Printing and related activities
	Class here book arts. For book illustration, see 741.6; publishing, 070; bibliography, 010
686.2	Printing
686.3	Bookbinding
686.4	Photocopying
687	Clothing
	Class here tailoring. For clothing manufacture in general, home clothing manufacture, see 646.4; leather and fur clothing manufacture, 685
688	Other final products, and packaging technology
	Examples: smokers' supplies, recreational equipment, toys
688.8	Packaging technology
690	**Building and related activities**
	For design and construction in general, see 720; structural engineering, 624.1
694	Wood construction. Carpentry
	Class other building materials at 690
696	Utilities
	Examples: plumbing, hot water supply. For heating, ventilating, air-conditioning, electric utilities, see 697
697	Heating, ventilating, air-conditioning, electric utilities

700 The arts

Fine, decorative, literary, performing, recreational arts. For book arts, see 686; for literary arts specifically, see 800

700.1–700.9	Standard subdivisions for the arts *Notation from Table 1*
701–709	Standard subdivisions for the visual arts *Notation from Table 1*
702	Miscellany *Class here techniques, forgery, preservation, restoration*
704	Iconography *Visual art that treats of specific subjects, e.g., religion, the human body*
708	Galleries, museums, private collections *Descriptions, guidebooks, catalogues*
709	Historical and geographical treatment
709.01–709.04	Periods of development *Prefer 709.3–709.9, specific continents, etc., e.g., French Renaissance art 709.44*
709.01	Early period to 499 A.D.
709.02	500–1499
709.024	Renaissance period, 1400–1499
709.03	Modern period, 1500–
709.04	20th century
709.3–709.9	Treatment by specific continent, country, locality *Add "Areas" notation 3–9 to base number 709, e.g., art of Australia 709.94*

710 Civic and landscape art

711	Area planning *Town and country planning. For landscape design, see 712*
712	Landscape design (Landscape architecture)

720 Architecture

Class here comprehensive works on design and construction. For building technology, see 690; structural engineering, 624.1

720.9	Historical and geographical treatment
	Class here, without subdivision, history of architecture in general. Add "Areas" notation 4–9 from Table 2 to base numbers 720.9 for description of architecture in specific places in the modern world, e.g., Italian architecture 720.945. For ancient, oriental, and modern architecture in general, see 722–724
722–724	Schools and styles
722	Ancient and Oriental architecture
	Ancient regardless of place, Oriental regardless of period. Class here architecture of Aztec and other American Indians
723	Mediaeval architecture, 300–1399
724	Modern architecture, 1400–
724.1	Early modern, 1400–1800
	Class here Renaissance architecture
724.2	19th century
724.9	20th century
725–728	Buildings by purpose
725	Public buildings
	Class here fortified buildings, e.g., castles; official residences. For religious buildings, see 726; educational and research buildings, 727; palaces, 728.8
726	Buildings for religious and related purposes
727	Educational and research buildings
728	Residential buildings
	For official residences, see 725; clergy residences, 726; educational residential buildings, 727
728.8	Large and elaborate private dwellings
	Examples: palaces, mansions
730	**Sculpture**
	Class at 730, without subdivision, plastic arts in general
730.9	Historical and geographical treatment
	Class at 730.9, without subdivision, history of sculpture in general. Add "Areas" notation 4–9 from Table 2 to base number 730.9 for history and description of sculpture in specific places in the modern world, e.g., Italian sculpture 730.945. For Oriental, ancient, mediaeval, and modern sculpture in general, see 732–735

732–735	Schools, styles, periods
732	Ancient, Oriental sculpture
	Ancient regardless of place, Oriental regardless of period. For Greek, Etruscan, Roman sculpture, see 733
733	Ancient Greek, Etruscan, Roman sculpture
734	Mediaeval sculpture, 500–1399
735	Modern sculpture
735.21	Early modern, 1400–1799
	Class here Renaissance sculpture
735.22	19th century
735.23	20th century
736–739	Other plastic arts
736	Carving and carvings
737	Numismatics and sigillography
	For paper money, see 769.55
738	Ceramic arts
	Examples: pottery, enamelling, mosaic work. For glass, see 748
739	Art metalwork
	For numismatics, see 737
739.2	Work in precious metals
739.7	Arms and armour
740	**Drawing. Decorative and minor arts**
741	Drawing and drawings
	For drawing and drawings by subject, see 743
741.5	Cartoons, comics, caricatures
741.6	Graphic design, illustration, commercial art
	Class specific type with the subject, e.g., prints 760
742	Perspective
743	Drawing and drawings by subject
	Examples: animal life, human figure
743.9	Collections of drawings by subject
	Add 001–999 to base number 743.9, e.g., religious subjects 743.92
745	**Decorative and minor arts**
	Class here folk art in general. For other decorative and minor arts, see 736–739; interior decoration, 747
745.1	Antiques
	Identification, collection, restoration, preservation. Class a specific kind with the subject, e.g., brasses 739; automobiles 629.2

745.2	Industrial art and design
	Creative design of mass-produced commodities.
	Class design of a specific commodity with the subject,
	e.g., furniture 684.1; automobiles 629.2
745.5	Handicrafts
	Creative work done by hand or with the aid of simple
	machines. For floral arts, see 745.9
745.51	In wood
	For wood carving, see 736
745.53	In leather and fur
745.54	In paper
	Class here pâpier maché
745.55	In shells
745.56	In metals
745.57	In rubber and plastics
745.58	From beads, found, and other objects
745.59	Making specific objects
	Class here handicrafts in composite materials
745.592	Toys, models, miniatures
745.593	Useful objects
	Examples: candles, lampshades
745.594	Decorative objects
	Examples: greeting cards, jewelry
745.6	Lettering, illumination, heraldic design
	For heraldry in general, see 929.6
745.9	Floral arts
746	**Textile arts and handicrafts**
	For home sewing and clothing, see 646.3; textile
	manufacturing, 677
746.2	Laces and related fabrics
746.3	Pictures, hangings, tapestries
746.4	Needlework and handwork
746.41	Weaving
746.43	Knitting, crocheting, tatting
746.44	Embroidery and needlepoint
746.46	Quilting and patchwork
746.6	Printing, painting, dyeing
746.7	Rugs and carpets
746.9	Other textile processes
747.	**Interior decoration**
	For textiles, see 746; furniture and accessories, 749
748	Glass
	For glass manufacturing, see 666; ceramic arts, 738

749	Furniture and accessories
	For selection of furniture for the home, see 645; furniture manufacture, 684.1; interior decoration, 747
750	**Painting and paintings**
	For historical and geographical treatment, see 759
751	Materials, methods, forms
	Examples: ink, tempera, oils
751.6	Conservation, preservation, restoration, routine care
751.7	Specific forms
	Examples: murals, miniatures
753	Painting and paintings of specific subjects
754	Subjects of everyday life
755	Religious subjects
756	Historical events
757	Human subjects
758	Other subjects
759	Historical and geographical treatment
	Class in 759.01–759.06 schools and styles not limited by place
759.01	Earliest times to 499 A.D.
759.02	500–1399
	Class here early Christian, Byzantine, Romanesque, Gothic, Mediaeval painting
759.03	1400–1599
	Class here Renaissance painting
759.04	1600–1799
	Class here baroque, rococo painting
759.05	1800–1899
759.06	1900–
759.1–759.9	Geographical treatment
	Class here at country level individual painters regardless of process, form, subject. See note at 759
759.1	United States and Canada
759.2	British Isles
759.3	Germany
759.4	France
759.5	Italy
759.6	Spain
759.92	Netherlands
	Class here Flemish painting

759.93–759.99	Other areas

759.93–759.99 Other areas
    Add "Areas" notation 3–9 to base number 759.9, e.g.,
    European painting 759.94, Mexican painting 759.972

760   **Graphic arts. Printmaking and prints**
    For drawing and drawings, see 741; painting and
    paintings, 750; photography and photographs, 770;
    printing, 686.2

761   Relief processes

763   Lithography
    For chromolithography, see 764

764   Serigraphy (Silk screen printing) and Chromolithography

765   Metal engraving

766   Mezzotinting, aquatinting, related processes
    Class here composite processes

767   Etching and drypoint

769   Prints

769.1   Collecting, reproduction, preservation, routine care of prints
    Class here comprehensive works on reproduction of
    paintings and drawings

769.5   Various specific forms of prints

769.55   Paper money

769.56   Postage stamps
    Class here philately

769.9   Historical and geographical treatment
    Regardless of process, representation, style, period.
    Add "Areas" notation 3–9 from Table 2 to base
    number 769.9, e.g., English printmakers
    769.942

770   **Photography and photographs**

771   Apparatus, equipment, material, processes

778   Specific fields and kinds of photography
    Examples: microphotography, aerial photography

778.5   Cinematography, and television photography

778.9   Photographs of specific subjects
    Add 001–999 to base number 778.9, e.g., religious
    subjects 778.92

780   **Music**

780.1–780.9   Standard subdivisions
    Apply standard subdivisions as modified here
    throughout 780–789

780.1	Philosophy and theory

780.1   Philosophy and theory
Class general principles, "theory of music" in 781

780.7   Study, teaching, performances
Including festivals, competitions, awards

781–788   Principles and instruments
Unless other instructions are given, class books on subjects that have two or more characteristics given in the schedules in the number coming last in the schedules, e.g., composition of sonatas for the piano 786.2. Class comprehensive works in 780, items on the works of and the biographies of an individual composer in 780.92

781   **General principles and musical forms**
Class here "theory of music"

781.1   Basic principles
Including appreciation

781.2   Elements of music
Including rhythm, pitch, harmony, tonality and atonality, counterpoint

781.3   Composition
Including arrangement

781.4   Techniques of music
Including sight and score reading, ear training, conducting, accompaniment, recording of music. Class techniques of composition in 781.3

781.5   Various specific kinds of music
Including music for specific days and seasons of the year; film, radio, television music; dance, ballet, and theatre music; music for debuts, weddings, funerals. For vocal theatre music, see 782.1

781.6   **Traditions of music**

781.62   **Folk music**

781.64   **Western popular music**
For rock, see 781.75; jazz, 781.76

781.65   Rock (Rock 'n' roll)

781.66   Jazz

781.68   Western art ("classical") music

781.7   **Sacred music**

781.71   Christian sacred music
Including music for specific Christian denominations. For music of the Christian church year, see 781.62; hymns and carols and other vocal forms, 782

781.72	Music of the Christian church year
781.723	Christmas
781.726	Holy Week
781.727	Easter Sunday
781.8	Musical forms

781.8 — Musical forms
Including sonata, symphony, concerto, suite, dance forms, theme and variation, fugue, nocturnes, marches

782–788   Instruments
The instruments (including human voice) or groups of instruments for which music is written or by which it is performed

782   **Vocal music**
For music for single voices, see 783

782.1–782.4   Vocal forms
Class comprehensive works in 782

782.1   Dramatic vocal forms. Operas
Including operettas, musicals

782.2   Non-dramatic vocal forms
Including cantatas, oratorios, liturgical chants. Class here sacred vocal forms. For services, see 782.3; secular forms, 782.4

782.27   Hymns
For carols, see 782.28

782.28   Carols

782.3   Services (Liturgy and ritual)

782.32   Christian services
Including mass, morning and evening prayer

782.4   Secular forms

782.42   Songs

782.5–782.9   Voices
Class here scores and parts of music for specific vocal groups. Class comprehensive works in 782, dramatic music in 782.1, works on specific vocal forms for specific vocal groups with the form in 782.1–782.4

782.5   Mixed voices
Class here choral music

782.6   Women's voices

782.7   Children's voices

782.8   Men's voices

782.9   Other types of voices
Including yodelling

783	Music for single voices. The voice
	Class dramatic vocal forms in 782.1, works on vocal forms for specific kinds of single voice in 782.1–782.4
783.1	Single voices in combination
	Including duets, trios
784–788	Instruments and their music
	Class comprehensive works in 784
784	**Instruments and instrumental ensembles**
	For specific instruments and their music, see 786–788
784.2	Full (Symphony) orchestra
784.8	Wind band
	Including marching band
785	Chamber music
786–788	Specific instruments and their music
	Class here music for solo instrument, music for solo instrument accompanied by one other instrument in a supporting role. Class comprehensive works in 784, chamber music in 785
786	Keyboard, mechanical, electrophonic, percussion instruments
	Class here comprehensive works on keyboard instruments
786.2	Pianos
786.5	Organs
786.7	Electronic music
786.8	Percussion instruments
	Including cymbals, bells. For drums, see 786.9
786.9	Drums
787	Stringed instruments. Bowed string instruments
	Including violas, cellos, zithers, lutes, harps. Class keyboard stringed instruments in 786
787.2	Violins
787.8	Guitars
788	Wind instruments
	Including woodwinds, e.g., flutes, oboes, clarinets, saxophones; brass instruments, e.g., trumpets, trombones, cornets, tubas. Class keyboard wind instruments in 786
790	**Recreational and performing arts**
	For music, see 780
790.1	**Recreational activities in general. Hobbies**
	Class here hobbies in general. For hobbies associated with a subject, see subject, e.g., music as a hobby 780

790.13	Activities generally engaged in by individuals
790.132	Collecting
	Class collecting particular kinds of objects with the subject, using "Standard subdivisions" notation –075 from Table 1, e.g., collecting furniture 749.075
790.133	Play with mechanical and scientific toys
	For computer games, see 794.8
790.134	Participation in contests. Competitions
790.138	Activities engaged in alone with a mediating element
	Examples; reading, watching, listening
790.19	Activities for specific groups
	Examples: for families, girls, invalids
790.2	The performing arts in general
	For music, see 780

791	**Public performances**
791.3	Circuses
791.4	Cinema (Motion pictures), radio, television
791.43	Cinema (Motion pictures)
791.44	Radio
791.45	Television
791.5	Puppet, miniature, toy theatres
791.6	Pageants, parades
791.8	Animal shows
	For circus animal performances, see 791.3; equestrian sports and animal racing, 798

792	**Theatre**
	For texts of plays, see 800
792.1	Tragedy and serious drama
792.2	Comedy, melodrama, suspense drama
792.3	Pantomine
792.7	Vaudeville, music hall, variety, cabaret, night club presentations
792.8	Ballet

793	**Indoor games and amusements**
	For indoor games of skill, see 794; games of chance, 795
793.2	Party games
	Examples: hunt the thimble, dumb crambo
793.3	Dancing
	For ballet, see 794.8
793.7	Puzzles, riddles, crosswords, mathematical games
	For computer games, see 794.8

793.8	Magic, juggling, ventriloquism, scientific recreations
794	Indoor games of skill
	For games combining skill and chance, see 795
794.1	Chess
794.2	Board games other than chess
	For backgammon, see 795.1
794.22	Draughts (Checkers)
794.3	Darts
794.6	Indoor bowling
794.7	Ball games
	Examples: billiards, pool, snooker. For indoor bowling, see 794.6
794.8	Electronic games. Computer games
795	Games of chance
	Class here gambling
795.1	Dice, wheel, counter, number games
	Examples: backgammon, roulette, dominoes, bingo, mah-jongg
795.4	Card games
795.41	Games dependent chiefly on skill
	Examples: bridge, whist
796	**Athletic and outdoor sports and games**
	For aquatic and air sports, see 797; equestrian sports and animal racing, 798; fishing, hunting, shooting, 799
796.1	Miscellaneous games
	Examples: singing games, kite flying, hopscotch
796.3	Ball games
796.32	Ball thrown or hit by hand
	Examples: basketball, lawn bowling, netball, volleyball
796.33	Ball propelled by foot
796.332	American football
796.333	Rugby football
796.334	Soccer (Association football)
796.335	Canadian football
796.34	Racket games
796.342	Tennis (Lawn tennis)
796.343	Rackets and squash
796.345	Badminton
796.347	Lacrosse
796.35	Ball driven by club, mallet, bat
796.352	Golf
796.353	Polo

796.354	Croquet
796.355	Field hockey
796.357	Baseball
796.358	Cricket
796.4	Athletic exercises and gymnastics
796.42	Track and field athletics
796.48	Olympic games
	Class a specific activity with the activity, e.g.,
	swimming 797.2. For Winter Olympics, see 796.98
796.5	Outdoor life
	Class here orienteering, beach sports
796.51	Walking
796.52	Mountaineering. Rock climbing
796.525	Caving. Potholing
796.54	Camping
796.6	Cycling
	Use of wheeled vehicles not driven by motor or
	animal power
796.7	Motor sports
	Use of wheeled motor vehicles
796.8	Combat sports
	Examples: boxing, fencing, karate, wrestling
796.9	Ice and snow sports
	Examples: skating, skiing, snowmobiling, ice hockey
796.98	Winter Olympic games
797	Aquatic sports and air sports
	For fishing, see 799.1
797.1	Boating. Sailing
	Class here racing
797.2	Swimming and diving
797.3	Other aquatic sports
	Examples: surfing, water skiing
797.5	Air sports
	Examples: parachuting, gliding, flying for pleasure,
	racing
798	Equestrian sports and animal racing
798.2	Horsemanship
798.4	Horse racing. Coaching
798.8	Racing animals other than horses
799	Fishing, hunting, shooting
799.1	Fishing
799.2	Hunting
799.3	Shooting other than game

118

800 Literature (Belles-lettres)

Works of and about literature. Class comprehensive works on language and literature in 400

808   Rhetoric (Composition) and collections
Class here authorship, preparation of manuscripts

808.1   Rhetoric of poetry

808.2   Rhetoric of drama

808.3   Rhetoric of fiction

808.4   Rhetoric of essays and prose

808.5   Rhetoric of speech
Class here voice, expression, gesture, elocution

808.51   Public speaking (Oratory)

808.53   Debating

808.54   Recitation, storytelling, reading aloud

808.7   Rhetoric of humour

808.8   Collections from more than one literature
Class collections of specific literatures in 810–890

808.81   Collections of poetry

808.82   Collections of drama

808.83   Collections of fiction

808.84   Collections of essays

808.85   Collections of speeches

808.87   Collections of wit and humour

808.88   Collections of miscellaneous writings, writings for specific groups

809   History, description, critical appraisal of general literature
Of more than one literature, e.g., history of the novel. For history, etc. of a specific literature or literature group, see 810–890

809.1–7   Literature in specific forms, miscellaneous forms, and for specific groups
Add to base number 809 the numbers following 808.8 in 808.81–808.88

810–890   Specific literatures
Literatures in specific languages or language groups. See Introduction, paragraph 13.2, for methods of distinguishing between different national outputs in the same language, e.g., French of Canada and French of France

With the exception of 810 and 839.09, the grouping follows exactly that in 420–490 (Languages). Replace initial 4 (430, German language) by an initial 8 (830, German literature)

The literature of languages indicated by an asterisk may be subdivided by adding "Subdivisions for individual literatures" (Table 3) to the base number which is the same as the class number unless otherwise indicated, e.g., *439.36 Afrikaans language, *839.36 Afrikaans literature, 839.361 Afrikaans poetry; *430 German language, base number 43, base number for German literature 83, German poetry 831. Further subdivision by period is possible. See Table 3

Class items by or about specific authors covering more than one form, with the form principally associated with the author, e.g., collected works of G. B. Shaw with drama (822), and in period during which writer was most active, e.g., for Shaw early twentieth century 822.912. Alternatively class in —8, 828.912

810	*American literature in English*

English language literature of the Western Hemisphere and Hawaii. Base: 81. Subdivide by using Table 3 and Table 3P

820	*English literature*

For Anglo-Saxon (Old English) see 829; American literature in English, 810. Base number: 82.
820.8–828 may be subdivided by adding notation from Table 3P, e.g., 820.83 Anthology of Elizabethan literature, 821.3 Elizabethan poetry

820.8	Collections

More than one form, more than one author. Example: Anthology of English literature

820.9	History, description, critical appraisal

More than one form, more than one author. Example: History of English literature

821	Poetry
822	Drama
823	Prose fiction (Novels, short stories)
824	Essays

Class here literary works. Class works on specific subjects with the subject

825	Speeches

Note as at 824

826	Letters

Note as at 824

120

827	Satire and humour
	Example: English satirical writers. However, prefer 821–826, e.g., English humourous poetry, 821
828	Miscellaneous writings
	Quotations, jokes, epigrams, experimental and non-formalized works. May be used for items by or about specific authors covering more than one form, e.g., collected works of Rudyard Kipling. See note at 810–890
829	*Anglo-Saxon literature
830	*German literature
	Subdivide by using Table 3. Base number: 83. Class here, without subdivision, Germanic literature in general
839.09	*Yiddish literature
840	*French literature
	Subdivide by using Table 3 and Table 3P. Base number: 84. Class here, without subdivision, Romance literatures in general
850	*Italian literature
	Subdivide by using Table 3. Base number: 85
860	*Spanish literature
	Subdivide by using Table 3. Base number: 86
870	*Latin literature
	Subdivide by using Table 3. Base number: 87
880	*Classical Greek literature
	Subdivide by using Table 3. Base number: 88
890	Literatures of other languages
	For literatures of specific languages, add to base number 89 the numbers following 49 in 491–499, e.g., Welsh literature 891.66

900   Geography, history and their auxiliaries
Unless otherwise instructed class geographical and historical treatment of a subject with the subject, using "Standard subdivisions" notation 09 from Table 1, e.g., history of agriculture 630.9; of science 509. See Introduction, section 14, for alternative ways of treating geography and history

904   Collected accounts of specific events and types of events
          Examples: revolution, accidents

909   World history. History of civilisation
          Not limited by location. Class here the history of specific groups of people irrespective of place, e.g., history of the English-speaking people. For general ancient history (to 500), see 930

909.07   Mediaeval period (500–1450)
909.08   Modern period (1450–)

910   General geography and travel
          Not limited by location. Prefer location, e.g., physical geography of Europe 914

910.02   Physical geography
          For specific areas, e.g., Australia, see 913–919; for specific kinds of areas, e.g., deserts, see 910.09. Prefer 913–919, e.g., deserts of Australia 919.94

910.09   Geography of, and travel in areas, regions, places in general
          Add "Areas" notation 1 from Table 2 to base number 910.09, e.g., geography of deserts, 910.09154

910.2   World travel guides
910.3   Dictionaries, encyclopaedias, gazetteers
910.9   Discovery and exploration
          Class specific areas explored in 913–919

910.93–910.99   Discovery and exploration by specific countries
          Add "Areas" notation 3–9 to base number 910.9, e.g., by Spain 910.946

911   Historical geography

912   Atlases and maps in general
912.1   Specific subjects and regions in general
          If preferred, class subject representations with subject, e.g., flight maps 629.1

912.19	Areas, regions, places in general
	Add to base number 912.19 the numbers
	following 1 in "Areas" notation 11–19 from
	Table 2, e.g., maps of the Atlantic region
	912.19821
912.3–912.9	Maps and atlases of specific continents, countries,
	localities, extraterrestrial worlds
	Add "Areas" notation 3–9 from Table 2 to base
	number 912, e.g., maps of South America 912.8.
	However, if preferred, class in 913, 914–919
913–919	Geography of, and travel in the ancient world; specific
	continents, countries, localities in the modern world;
	extraterrestrial worlds
	Add "Areas" notation 3–9 from Table 2 to base
	number 91, e.g., Australia 919.4. Class here
	discovery and exploration, e.g., discovery of Mexico
	917.2. For discovery and exploration by specific
	countries, see 910.93–910.99

920	**General biography. Genealogy. Names. Insignia**
	Class here biography, autobiography, diaries,
	reminiscences, correspondence. If preferred, class
	biography etc. of persons associated with a subject with
	the subject, using "Standard subdivisions" notation 092
	from Table 1, e.g., biographies of chemists 540.92. For
	biography etc. considered as literary art, see Table 3,
	biographies of writers considered as literary criticism,
	800
920.03–920.09	General collections of biography by place
	Add "Areas" notation 3–9 from Table 2 to base number
	920.0, e.g., collected biography of Canadians
	920.071

929	**Genealogy. Names. Insignia**
929.1	Genealogy. Family histories
929.4	Personal names
929.6	Heraldry
929.7	Royal houses, nobility, gentry, orders of knighthood
929.8	Awards, orders, decorations, autographs
929.9	Other forms of insignia and identification
	Examples: flags, non-personal names, license
	· *plates*

| 930–990 | History of the ancient world; specific continents, countries, localities of the modern world; extraterrestrial worlds |
| | *Add "Areas" notation 3–9 to base number 9, e.g., history of Europe 940, of London 942.1 Class comprehensive works on ancient and modern world in 909, but for specific continents etc. prefer 940–990, e.g., history of ancient and modern Egypt 962. Class numbers for all continents and a selection of countries have been synthesized and are listed here, with period divisions in some cases. Extensions of these subdivisions and period subdivisions for other countries etc. can be obtained from the schedules of the unabridged edition. Note that starting and terminal dates are approximate* |

930	**History of the ancient world to 500 A.D.**
930.1	Archaeology
931	China to 420 A.D.
932	Egypt to 640 A.D.
933	Palestine to 70 A.D.
934	India to 647 A.D.
935	Mesopotamia and the Iranian plateau to 637 A.D.
936	Europe other than Greece and Italy to 500 A.D.
936.1	British Isles to 410 A.D. Roman Britain
936.3	Germanic regions to 481 A.D.
	For British Isles, see 936.1
936.4	Celtic region to ca. 486 A.D.
	For British Isles, see 936.1
936.6	Iberian peninsula and adjacent islands
937	Italian peninsula and adjacent territories to 476 A.D.
	Class here Roman empire. For comprehensive works on Greece and Rome, see 938
938	Greece to 323 A.D.
	Class here Macedonian empire; comprehensive works on Greece and Rome
939	Other parts of the ancient world
	For parts of Africa and Asia not covered in 930 and subdivisions, and for all North and South America, see 940–990
940–990	History of specific continents, countries, localities of the modern world from 500 A.D.; extraterrestrial worlds
	For starting dates of specific continents etc., see terminal dates in 930; but if preferred, class here ancient history subdivision 01 if period is to be specified

940	Europe
	Class here without subdivision Western Europe
940.1	Early history to 1453
940.2	Modern history, 1453–
940.21	Renaissance period, 1453–1517
940.22	Reformation to French Revolution, 1517–1789
940.23	Reformation period, 1517–1648
940.25	Late 17th to mid-18th century, 1648–1789
940.27	Napoleonic era, 1789–1815
940.28	19th century, 1815–1914
940.3	World War I, 1914–1918
940.5	20th century, 1918–
	For World War I, see 940.3
940.51	1918–1939
940.53	World War II 1939–1945
940.55	1945–

941	**British Isles, United Kingdom, Great Britain**
941.01	Early history to 1066
941.02	12th century
941.03	13th and 14th century
941.04	15th century
941.05	16th century
941.06	17th century
	Class here the Stuarts, the Commonwealth
941.07	18th century
	Class here Hanoverian dynasty
941.08	Victoria and House of Windsor, 1837–
941.081	Victoria, 1837–1901
941.082	Edward VII, 1901–1910
941.083	George V, 1910–1936
941.084	1936–1952
	Class here reigns of Edward VIII, George VI
941.085	1952–
	Class here reign of Elizabeth II
941.1	Scotland
941.101	Early history to 1057
941.102	12th and 13th centuries
941.103	14th century
941.104	1424–1542
941.105	Reformation period, 1542–1602

941.106–941.108	Union with England to the present
	Divide like 941.06–941.08, e.g., United Kingdom, reign of George V, 941.083; Scotland, reign of George V, 941.1083
941.5	Ireland
941.501	Early history to 1086
941.502	12th century
941.503	13th and 14th centuries
	Class here Plantagenet period
941.504	15th century
	Class here Lancaster and York periods
941.505	16th century
	Class here Tudor period
941.506	17th century
	Class here Stuart and Commonwealth periods
941.507	18th century
941.508	19th and 20th centuries
941.5081	19th century
941.5082	20th century
941.6	Ulster. Northern Ireland
941.608	19th and 20th centuries
941.6081	19th century
941.6082	20th century
941.7	Eire (Republic of Ireland)
941.708	19th and 20th centuries
941.7081	19th century
941.7082	20th century
942	England and Wales
	For Wales, see 942.9
942.01	Early history to 1066
942.02	1066–1154
942.03	1154–1399 (Plantagenets)
942.04	1399–1485 (Lancaster and York)
942.05	1485–1603 (Tudors)
942.06–942.08	Union with Scotland to the present
	Divide like 941.06–941.08, e.g., United Kingdom, reign of George V, 941.083; England and Wales, reign of George V, 942.083; Wales, early period, 942.901
942.9	Wales
	Divide like 942, e.g., England and Wales, reign of George V, 942.083; Wales, reign of George V, 942.9083; Wales, early period, 942.901

943	**Germany**
	Class here without subdivision Central Europe, Holy Roman Empire
943.01	Early period to 843
943.02	843–1519
943.03	1519–1618
	Class here Reformation and Counter-Reformation
943.04	17th century
943.05	18th century
943.06	Napoleonic period, 1790–1866
943.08	1866–
943.081	1866–1918
943.085	1918–1933
943.086	1933–1945 (Third Reich)
943.087	1945–
	Class here Germany as a whole, Federal Republic of Germany. For German Democratic Republic, see 943.1
943.1	German Democratic Republic, 1945–
944	**France**
944.01	Early history to 987
944.02	987–1589
944.03	1587–1789 (Bourbons)
944.04	Revolution, 1789–1804
944.05	First Empire, 1804–1815
	For Napoleonic Wars, see 940.27
944.06	1815–1870
944.08	1870–
944.081	Third Republic, 1870–1945
944.082	Fourth Republic, 1945–1958
944.083	Fifth Republic, 1958–
945	**Italy**
945.01	Early history to 1300
945.05	Renaissance period, 1300–1494
945.06	1494–1796
945.08	1796–1870
945.09	1870–
945.091	1918–1946
945.092	1946–

946	Spain
946.01	Early period to 711
946.02	711–1516
	Moorish period, reconquest, Ferdinand and Isabella
946.05	1516–1808
	Class here Hapsburgs and Bourbons. For Bourbon restoration, see 946.07
946.06	1808–1814
	Period of War of Independence (Peninsular War)
946.07	1814–1868
	Bourbon restoration
946.08	1868–
946.081	1931–1975
	Second Republic, Civil War, Regime of Francisco Franco
946.083	1975–

947	**Union of Soviet Socialist Republics. Russia**
	Class here without subdivision Eastern Europe in general. For U.S.S.R. in Asia, see Table 2 —57, —58
947.01	Early history to 862
947.02	862–1725
	Class here Peter the Great
947.06	1725–1796
	Class here Catherine the Great
947.07	1796–1855
947.08	1855–
947.081	1855–1917
947.084	1917–1953
	Class here Revolutions, 20th century
947.085	1953–

| 948 | **Scandinavia** |
| 949 | **Other parts of Europe** |

950	**Asia**
954	India
	Class here the Indian sub-continent, India under British Rule (The British Raj), the Indian state after British Rule
954.04	1947–
954.91	Pakistan, 1947–
	For East Bengal (Bangladesh), see 954.92
954.92	Bangladesh, 1947–

| 954.93 | Sri Lanka (Ceylon) |
| 954.9303 | 1948– |

960 **Africa**
960.1	Early history to 640
960.2	640–1945
960.3	1945–

970 **North and Central America**

971 **Canada**
971.01	Earliest times to 1763
971.02	1763–1791
971.03	1791–1841
971.04	1841–1867
971.05	1867–1911
971.06	1911–
971.061	1911–1921
971.062	1921–1935
971.063	1935–1957
971.064	1957–

972	Mexico
972.8	Central America
972.9	West Indies and Bermuda

973 **United States**
For Hawaii, see 996
973.1	Earliest times to 1607
973.2	1607–1775
973.3	1775–1789
973.4	1789–1809
973.5	1809–1845
973.6	1845–1861
973.7	1861–1865 (Civil War)
973.8	1865–1901
973.9	1901–
973.92	1953–

980 **South America**
Class here without subdivision Spanish America, Latin America in general. For Mexico, Central America, and the West Indies, see 972

990	Other parts of the world. Extraterrestrial worlds
993	**New Zealand and Melanesia**
993.1	**New Zealand**
993.101	Earliest times to 1840
993.102	1860–1908
993.103	1908–
993.1031	1908–1918
993.1032	1918–1945
993.1035	1945–1969
993.1037	1969–
994	**Australia**
994.01	Earliest times to 1788
994.02	1788–1851
994.03	1851–1901
994.04	1901–1945
994.05	1945–1965
994.06	1965–
995	**Papua New Guinea**
996	Other parts of the Pacific
	Class here Hawaii

Alphabetical Subject Index

ALPHABETICAL SUBJECT INDEX

Alphabetical index to schedule and tables
Entries for complete and summary schedules and for the tables are in one alphabetical sequence.

Summary schedules
Where the class number for complete and summary schedules differs, the class number for the latter is given in parentheses. Examples:

Abnormal psychology   157 (150)
Anglican Churches   283 (280/283)

In the second example, 280 is the general class number for denominations and sects of the Christian Church, as distinct from the Anglican Churches specifically. There is an indication at 280 in the summary schedules to "select as required class numbers from complete schedules" (in this case 283) for a denomination of local interest. This number is provided after the slash mark (see Introduction to summary schedules).

No special summary numbers are provided for the tables, which, it is assumed, will be used with the complete schedules only.

The tables
In the index, the numbers for the tables are preceded by a dash (e.g., −09). This dash is NOT part of the notation. It represents a blank which must be filled by a number from the schedules.

Classes and terms included in the index
Most listed terms and some other frequently sought terms are included in the index. Classes to be derived by synthesis and not indexed can be added as required at the local level, as can locally important synonyms and specifics (see Introduction, 5.11–5.14, 15.3).

Period classes identified by number only (e.g., sixteenth century) are not indexed, although verbally named periods (e.g., Renaissance) may be. (Numbered periods always appear in chronological order in the schedules or tables under what will almost certainly be the main sought class, e.g., English history.) However, entries for numbered periods can be made at the local level.

Contexts

The index is a *relative* index in that terms are placed in the context of a superordinate class (see Introduction, 5.11). However, the context is not given if the term occurs only once and/or the context is obvious.

Examples:

Anarchism	
Political science	321 (320)
Anglo-Saxon literature	829

"Anarchism" and "Anglo-Saxon literature" each occur only once, but "anarchism" might occur within philosophy and sociology as well as political science, whereas "Anglo-Saxon literature" belongs "naturally" to literature.

Inversion and synonyms

Some adjective noun phrases are inverted and some are not. The direct form is used where the phrase is, in effect, a compound word, or where the noun has little significance without the adjective, e.g., "Bibliographic control," which has little relationship to "arms control," "self control," etc. It is also used where—although the noun retains its significance—the term has become a widely known consensus term likely to be sought on first "look-up," e.g., "analytical chemistry." The inverted form is used when these conditions do not apply or where the use of the direct form would result in an inconvenient degree of scatter, e.g., "Animals, food," "Animals, working." Access through alternative forms is provided where necessary by duplicate entry (see Introduction, 5.11, on synonyms).

Filing order

The filing order is word-by-word rather than letter-by-letter; initials are filed as if each is a separate word. Examples:

Book collecting	EEC
Bookbinding	Education

A

Ability | 153 (150)
Abnormal psychology | 157 (150)
medicine | 616.89 (610)
Abstinence | 178 (170)
Abstracting (Summarizing) | 025 (020)
Abused children | 362.7(362)
Abyssinia | T.2–63
Academic achievement | 371.3
Accident prevention | 363.1
Accidents | 904 (900)
Accordions | 786 (784)
Accountancy | 657 (651)
Acoustics
building | 690
engineering | 620.2 (620)
physics | 534
Acrostics | 793.7
| (793 / 793.7)
Acting | 791.4 (791)
Acts of the Apostles | 226 (225)
Actuarial science | 368 (360)
Adaptive mechanisms
(animals) | 591.5 (591)
Addictions
ethics | 178 (170)
medicine | 613.8 (613)
psychology | 157 (150)
social welfare | 362.29 (362)
Administration (Govt.) | 350
Admirals | 359.092 (355)
Admiralty Islands | T.2–932
Adolescence
medicine | 618.92 (610)
psychology | 155 (150)
social welfare | 362.7 (362)
sociology | 305.2 (305)
Adoption
social welfare | 362.8 (362)
Adult education | 374 (370)
Advent | 263 (230)
Adventist churches | 286 (280/286)
Advertising | 659
Aegean Sea Islands | T.2–499
Aerial photography | 778 (770)
Aeronautical engineering | 629.1
Aeronautics | 629.1
Aerospace engineering | 629.1
Aerospace transportation | 387.7
Aesthetics | 700
philosophy | 100
Afghanistan | T.2–58
Africa
area number | T.2–6
history | 960
regional associations | 341.249 (340)

African languages | 496 (400 / 496)
See also Afro-Asiatic
languages
Afrikaans language | 439.36
| (400 / 439.36)
Afro-Asiatic languages | 492 (400 / 492)
Age groups
sociology | 305.2 (305)
Aged persons
medicine | 618.92
psychology | 155 (150)
social welfare | 362.2 (362)
sociology | 305.2
Ageism | 305.2 (305)
Agnosticism | 210 (200)
Agricultural equipment | 631.2 (630)
Agriculture | 630
Aid to the needy
international politics | 327 (320)
social welfare | 362
Air-conditioning | 697 (690)
Air forces and air combat | 358 (355)
Air pollution
social problem | 363.73 (363.7)
Air sports | 795.5
| (796 / 797.5)
Air transportation | 387.7
safety | 363.124(363.1)
Air warfare | 358 (355)
Aircraft
military science | 358 (355
technology | 629.1
transportation | 387.73 (387.7)
Airplanes
military science | 358 (355)
technology | 629.1
transportation | 387.73 (387.7)
Airports | 387.73 (387)
Alabama (U.S.A.) | T.2–76
Alaska (U.S.A.) | T.2–79
Albania | T.2–496
Albanian language | 491.9
| (400 / 491.9)
Alberta (Canada) | T.2–712
Alcohol
chemical technology | 663 (660)
Alcohol addiction
ethics | 178 (170)
medicine | 613.8 (613)
psychology | 157 (150)
social welfare | 362.29 (362)
Algae | 588 (580 / 588)
Algebra | 512
Algeria | T.2–65
Alienation | 302.5 (302)
Aliens
economics | 331.1 (331)
political science | 323 (320)

135

Alkalis	661 (660)	conservation	590.7
Allah (Islam)	297.2 (290)	diseases	
Alligators	597.9	veterinary medicine	636.089 (636)
	(591/597.9)	zoology	591.1 (591)
Allopathy	615.5 (610)	ecology	591.5 (591)
Alloys	620.1	experiments (Medicine)	619 (610)
Almanacs (Astronomy)	529	legends	398.24 (398)
Almanacs (Reference books)	030	lore	398.24 (398)
Alphabets	411 (400)	maturation	591.3 (591)
America		performances	
area number	T.2–7	(entertainment)	791.8 (791)
history	970	physiology	591.1 (591)
painters	759.1 (750)	psychology	591.5 (591)
philosophers	191 (190)	reproduction	591.3 (591)
regional associaitons	341.245 (340)	sports	798–799
American football	796.332		(796/798–799)
	(796/796.332)	sounds	591.5 (591)
American literature	810	training	636.08 (636)
American native languages	497–498	treatment of	
	(400/497–498)	ethics	179 (170)
American Reformed Church	285 (280/285)	hunting	175 (170)
Amerindian languages	497–498	zoology	591
	(400/497–498)	Animals, Extinct	591.04
Amphibians	597.6	Animals, Food	
	(591/597.6)	animal husbandry	636
Amusements	793	economic zoology	591.6 (591)
Anaesthetics	617 (610)	Animals, Pet	
Analysis (Mathematics)	515	animal husbandry	636
Analytical chemistry	543 (540)	economic zoology	591.6 (591)
Anarchism		Animals, Rare	591.04
political science	321 (320)	Animals, Working	
Anatomy	574.1	animal husbandry	636
animals	591.1 (591)	economic zoology	591.6 (591)
human	611 (612)	Animism	210 (200)
plant	581.1 (580)	Antarctic Ocean	T.2–167
Ancient history	930	Antarctica	T.2–989
Ancient philosophers	180 (100)	Antennas (Electronics)	621.384
Ancient sculpture	732 (730)		(621.38)
Ancient world	T.2–3	Anthologies and	
Andaman Islands		collections	
(India)	T.2–548	literature	808 (800)
Andhra Pradesh		specific literatures	T.2–08
(India)	T.2–548	Anthropology	301
Angels		Anthropology, Social and	
Christianity	235 (230)	cultural	306 (301)
Anglican churches	283 (280/283)	Anthropology, Physical	573
Anglo-Saxon language	429	Antibiotics	615 (610)
Anglo-Saxon literature	829	Antigua	T.2–7297
Angola	T.2–67	Antiques	745.1 (745)
Anguilla	T.2–7297	Antrim (N. Ireland)	T.2–4161
Animal husbandry	636	Ants	595.7
Animal shows	791.8 (791)		(591/595.7)
Animals		Apartheid	320
adaptation	591.5 (591)	Apes	599.8
agriculture	636		(591/599.8)
behaviour	591.5 (591)	Apiaries	638
collections	590.7	Apocalyptic literature	228 (225)
communication	591.5 (591)	Apocrypha	229

Apodiformes	598.8 (591/598.8)	Arts and crafts	745.5 (745)
Apostles, Acts of the	226 (225)	Aruba	T.2–7298
Apparitions	133.1 (130)	Arunachal (India)	T.2–541
Appearance, Physical	646.71 (646.7)	Asia	
Appliances, Household		area number	T.2–5
home economics	643	history	950
manufacture	683 (680)	philosophers	180 (100)
Applied mathematics	519	regional associations	341.247 (340)
Applied physics	621	Asia Minor	T.2–561
Applied psychology	158 (150)	Assam (India)	T.2–541
Applied sciences	600	Assamese language	491.46 (400/491.46)
Approximations (Mathematics)	511 (510)	Assassinations	364
Aptitude testing		Asses	
psychology	153.9 (150)	animal husbandry	636.1 (636/636.1)
Aquatic biology	574.92 (574)	zoology	599.725 (591/599.725)
Aquatic birds	598.3 (591/598)	Association football	796.334 (796/796.334)
Aquatic sports	797 (796/797)	Associations and clubs	366
Aquatinting	766 (760)	Christianity	267 (230)
Arab League	341.247 (340)	other religions See 290	
Arabian Peninsula	T.2–53	Assyria	T.2–35
Arabic language	492.7 (490/492.7)	history	935 (930)
Archaeology	930.1 (930)	Astrology	133.5 (13)
Architecture	720	Astronautical engineering	629.4
Archive administration	020	Astronautics	629.4
Arctic, Canadian	T.2–719	Astronomy	520
Arctic Ocean	T.2–1632	Astrophysics	523 (520)
Ards (N. Ireland)	T.2–4165	Atheism	210 (200)
Area planning	711 (710)	Athletics	796
Argentina	T.2–82	Atlantic Ocean	T.2–163
history	982 (980)	Atlantic Ocean islands	T.2–97
Aristotle	182 (100)	Atlantic Ocean region	T.2–1821
Arithmetic	513	Atlantis (Myth)	398.23 (398)
Arizona (U.S.A.)	T.2–79	Atlases	912
Arkansas (U.S.A.)	T.2–76	Atmosphere	T.2–161
Armadilloes	599.3 (591/599.3)	meteorology	551.5
Armagh (N. Ireland)	T.2–4166	Atomic bomb	
Armies and land combat	356 (355)	military science	355.4 (355)
Arms and armour		technology	623.4 (623)
art metalwork	739.7 (730)	Atomic energy	
See also Firearms		hazards	363.17 (363.1)
Arrangement (Music)	781.3 (781)	technology	621.48
Art	700	Atomic physics	593.7 (539)
Religious significance (Christian)	246 (230)	Atomic warfare	355.4 (355)
Art collections	708 (700)	Auckland (New Zealand)	T.2–9312
Art metalwork	739.7 (730)	Audio-visual materials	T.1–0208
Arthur, King	398.22 (398)	Audiology	617.8 (610)
Artificial intelligence	005 (004)	Auditing	657 (650)
Artificial languages	499.9 (400/499.9)	Australia	T.2–94
		history	994
Artificial satellites		Australian Capital	
astronautics	629.4	Territory	T.2–947
Artists	709.2	Australian languages	499 (400/499)
		Austria	T.2–436

Authors	809.2 (800)	Ballet	
Authorship	800	music	781.5 (781)
Autobiography	920	theatre	792.8 (792)
specific subjects	T.1–092	Ballistic missiles	
Autocracy		military science	355.4 (355)
political science	321 (320)	technology	623.4 (623)
Autographs	929.8 (929)	Balloons	
Automatic control		sports	797.5
data processing	004		(796/797.5)
engineering	629.8	Ballymena (N. Ireland)	T.2–4161
Autonomic nervous		Ballymoney (N. Ireland)	T.2–4161
system	612.88 (612)	Baltic languages	491.9
Automation			(400/491.9)
engineering	629.8	Baltic states	T.2–47
specific subjects	s.s–028	Banbridge (N. Ireland)	T.2–4165
Automobile driving		Band music (Wind)	784.8 (784)
law	343 (340)	Bangladesh	T.2–5492
technology	629.2	Banking	332.1 (332)
Automobile engineering	629.2	Bankruptcy	346 (340)
Automobile sports	796.7	Bantu languages	496 (400/496)
	(796/796.7)	Baptism	
Automobiles	692.2	Christian worship	265 (230)
Aves See Birds		Baptist churches	286 (280/286)
Aviaries	598.07	Barbados	T.2–7298
Avon (County) England	T.2–423	Bargaining (Labour)	331.8 (331)
Awards and decorations	929.8 (929)	Barns	631.2 (630)
Azores (Portugal)	T.2–469	Baroque painting	759.04 (750)
Aztecs	972	Barter	332.4 (332)
		Baseball	796.357
B			(796/796.357)
		Basketball	796.32
Baboons	599.8		(796/796.32)
	(591/599.8)	Basketmaking	746.41 (746)
Baby foods	641.3 (641)	Basotho-Qwaqwa	
Babylonian Empire	T.2–35	(S. Africa)	T.2–6859
Babysitting	649	Basque language	499 (400/499)
Backgammon	795.1	Basutoland (S. Africa)	T.2–6816
	(753/795.1)	Battered children	362.7 (362)
Bacteria	589.9	Battles	909 (900)
	(580/589.9)	See also specific wars	
Bacteriology	589.9	Beach sports	796.5
	(580/589.9)		(796/796.5)
Badminton (Game)	796.345 (796)	Beadwork	745.58
Bahaism	299 (290/299)		(745/745.58)
Bahamas	T.2–7296	Bears	
Bahasa Malay lang.	499.2	zoology	599.74
	(400/499.2)		(591/599.74)
Bahrain	T.2–53	Beauty culture	646.71 (646.7)
Baking	641.6 (641)	Bechuanaland	T.2–6811
Balance of trade	382 (380.1)	Bedfordshire (England)	T.2–425
Balinese language	499.2	Beef cattle	636.2 (636)
	(400/499.2)	Beekeeping	638
Balkan Peninsula	T.2–496	Beetles	595.7
Ball games, Indoor	794.7		(591/595.7)
	(793/794.7)	Behaviour	
Ball games, Outdoor	796.3	animals	591.5 (591)
	(796/796.3)	etiquette	395
Ballads	T.3–1	sociology	301

138

Behavioural sciences	300	palaeozoology	568 (560)
Belfast (N. Ireland)	T.2–4167	zoology	598
Belgium	T.2–492	Birds, Extinct	598.04
Belize	T.2–7282		(591 / 598.04)
Belles-lettres	800	Birds of prey	598.9
Bells, Musical	786.8 (786)		(591 / 598.9)
Bengal, East	T.2–5492	Birth control	
Bengal, West (India)	T.2–541	ethics	176 (170)
Bengali language	491.45	techniques	613.9 (613)
	(400 / 491.45)	Birth customs	392 (390)
Benin	T.2–66	Bismarck Archipelago	T.2–932
Berber language	493 (400 / 493)	Bison	
Berkshire (England)	T.2–422	animal husbandry	636.2
Berlin (Germany)	T.2–4315		(636/636.2)
Bermuda	T.2–7299	sociology	599.73
Betting			(591/599.73)
ethics	175 (170)	Black Africa	T.2–67
gaming	795 (793)	Blacks	
Beverages		social group	305.9 (305)
home economics	641.2 (640)	Blacksmithing	682 (680)
technology	663 (660)	Bleaching	
Bhutan	T.2–5498	technology	667 (660)
Bible	220	Blindness	
Bible stories	220.9 (220)	medicine	617.7 (610)
Bibliographic control	025 (020)	social welfare	362.41 (362)
Bibliographies	011	Blood	
subject	016 (011)	diseases	616.4 (610)
Bibliography		physiology	612.1 (612)
(Compiling)	T.2–025 (020)	Board games	794.2
Bicycles			(793 / 794.2)
engineering	629.2	Boating	797.1
sport	796.6		(796 / 797.1)
	(796 / 796.6)	Boats (Naval)	
transport	388.3 (388)	naval engineering	623.8
Bihar (India)	T.2–541	transportation	387.2 (387)
Bihari language	491.46	Body, Human	611 (612)
	(400 / 491.46)	Boiling (Cooking)	641.6 (641.5)
Bilingual dictionaries	T.4–3	Bolivia	T.2–84
Billiards	794.7	Bonaire	T.2–7298
	(793 / 794.7)	Bones, Human	
Biochemistry	574.19 (574.1)	anatomy	611 (612)
human	612.015 (612)	diseases and injuries	616.7 (610)
Biography	920	physiology	612.4 (612)
specific subjects	T.1–092	Book arts	686 (680)
Biological resources		Book catalogues	011 (011)
conservation	639.9 (639)	subject	016 (011)
economics	333.9 (333)	Book collecting	010
Biology	574	Bookbinding	686.3 (680)
Bionics	005 (004)	Bookkeeping	657 (651)
Biophysics	574.19 (574.1)	Books	010
human	612.014 (612)	Boolean algebra	511.3
Bird banding	598.07 (590.7)	Bophuthatswana	
Bird watching	598.07 (590.7)	(S. Africa)	T.2–6829
Birds		Borders, Scottish	T.2–413
animal husbandry	636.6	Borrowing	332.7 (332)
	(636/636.6)	Botanical gardens	580.7
hunting	799.2	Botanical sciences	580
	(796/799.2)	Botany	581 (580)

139

Bottles
  ceramic arts 738 (730)
  glass arts 748 (745)
  manufacture 666 (660)
Botswana T.2–6811
Bourbon dynasty
  France 944.03 (944)
  Spain 946.05 (946)
Bouvet Island T.2–971
Bovines
  animal husbandry 636.2
    (636/636.2)
  zoology 599.7
    (591/599.7)
Bowed instruments
  (Music) 787 (784/787)
Bowling, Indoor 794.6
    (793/794.6)
Bowling, Lawn 796.32
    (796/796.32)
Boxing (Sport) 796.8 (796)
Boys' clubs 366
  specific subjects T.1–06
Brahmanism 294.5
    (290/294.5)
Brain
  diseases and injuries 616.8 (610)
  physiology 612.82 (612)
Brass instruments
  (Music) 788 (784/788)
Brazil T.2–81
Breeding habits
  (Animals) 591.3 (591)
Breeding of animals 636.08 (636)
Breton language 491.68
    (400/491.68)
Bridge (Game) 795.41
    (793/795.41)
Bridges 624.2 (624)
Britain See British Isles
British Columbia T.2–711
British Commonwealth T.2–171241
British Empire 941
British Guiana T.2–881
British Honduras T.2–7282
British Isles
  ancient area number T.2–361
  modern area number T.2–41
  history to 5th century A.D. 936.1
    (930/936.1)
  history from 5th century
    A.D. 941
  painters 759.2 (750)
  philosophers 192 (100)
Broadcasting 791.4 (791)
Brooms 679 (670)
Brunei T.2–595
Bryophyta 588 (581/588)

Buckinghamshire (Eng.) T.2–425
Buddhism 294.3
    (290/294.3)
Building 690
Buildings
  architecture 720
  building technology 690
Bulgaria T.2–4977
Bureaucracies 302.3 (302)
Burial 392
Burma T.2–591
Burundi T.2–67
Business 658
Business law 346 (340)
Byzantine architecture 723 (720)
Byzantine art 709.02 (700)
  painting 759.02 (750)

C

Cabarets 792.7 (792)
Cacti 583 (580/583)
Calculating machines
  computer science 004
  office management 651.2 (651)
Calculus 515
Calendars 529
California (U.S.A.) T.2–794
Calligraphy 754.6
    (745/745.6)
Calvinist churches 284 (280/284)
Cambodia T.2–596
Cambridgeshire
  (England) T.2–426
Cameras 770
Cameroon T.2–67
Camouflage 355.4 (355)
Camping 796.54
    (796/796.54)
Canada
  area number T.2–71
  history 971
  painters 759.1 (750)
  philosophers 191 (100)
Canadian Arctic T.2–719
Canals
  engineering 627
  transportation 386.4 (386)
Canary Islands T.2–649
Canberra (Australia) T.2–947
Cancer
  medicine 616.9 (610)
Canning and preserving 641.4 (641)
Canoeing 797.1
    (796/797.1)
Canyons T.2–144
Cape of Good Hope
  (South Africa) T.2–687

140

Cape Verde T.2–66

Capital punishment
  criminology 364
  ethics 179 (170)

Capitalism 330.1 (330)

Caprimulgiformes 598.9
  (591 / 598.9)

Card games 795.4
  (793 / 795.4)

Cardinals (Birds) 599.8
  (591 / 599.8)

Cardiovascular diseases 616.1
  (610 / 616.1)

Career guides
  education 371.4

Careers 331 (330)

Caricatures 741.5 (740)

Carnivores 599.74
  (591 / 599.74)

Carols (Christian music) 782.28 (782)

Carpentry 694 (690)

Carpets and rugs
  buildings 690
  home economics 643.3 (643)

Carriacou T.2–7298

Carrickfergus
  (N. Ireland) T.2–4161

Cartography 526.8

Cartoons 741.5 (740)

Carving 736 (730)

Castlereagh (N. Ireland) T.2–4165

Castles
  architecture 725 (720)

Catalogues, Book 011
  subject 016 (011)

Catalogues,
  Commercial T.1–029

Cataloguing (Librarianship) 025 (020)

Catechisms
  Christianity 238 (230)
  other religions 290

Cathedrals 726 (720)

Catholic churches 282 (280 / 282)

Cats
  animal husbandry 636.8 (636)
  pets 636.8 (636)
  zoology 599.74
  (591 / 599.74)

Cattle 636.2 (636)

Causation 122 (100)

Cavan (Republic of
  Ireland) T.2–4169

Caves T.2–144
  exploring 796.525
  (796 / 796.525)

Cayman Islands T.2–7292

Celestial bodies 523 (520)

Celestial navigation 527

Celibacy
  ethics 176 (170)
  sociology 306.7 (306)

Cellos 787 (784)

Cells 574.8 (574)

Cellular biology 574.8 (574)

Cellular botany 581.8 (580)

Cellular zoology 591.8 (591)

Celtic languages 491.6
  (400 / 491.6)

Celtic regions T.2–364
  history to 600 A.D. 936.4
  (930 / 936.4)

Cemeteries
  burial custom 392 (390)
  haunted 133.1 (130)

Census records 310

Central African
  Republic T.2–67

Central America T.2–728

Central Asia T.2–58

Central Australia T.2–942

Central governments
  administration 351 (350)

Ceramics
  art 738 (730)
  technology 666 (660)

Cereals
  agriculture 633

Cetacea 599.5
  (591 / 599.5)

Chad T.2–67

Chad languages 493 (400 / 493)

Chamber music 785 (784)

Chance
  mathematics 519
  philosophy 122 (100)

Chance, Games of 795 (793 / 795)

Channel Islands
  (British Isles) T.2–4234

Chapbooks 398.5

Character 155 (150)

Charities 361.7 (361)

Charm 646.7

Charts See Maps

Checkers 794.22
  (793 / 794.22)

Chemical, Analytical 543 (540)

Chemical apparatus,
  Equipment 542 (540)

Chemical engineering 660.2 (660)

Chemical technologies 660

Chemicals, Industrial 661 (660)

Chemistry 540

Cheshire (England) T.2–427

Chess 794.1
  (793 / 794.1)

Chickens 636.5 (636)

Child abuse
  criminology 364
  social welfare 362.7 (362)
Child development
  psychology 155 (150)
  sociology 305.2 (305)
Child psychology 155 (150)
Child rearing 649.1 (649)
Childbirth 618.1 (610)
Children
  diseases 618.92 (610)
  social welfare 362.7 (362)
Children's literature 808 (800)
Children's voices (Music) 782.7 (782)
Chile T.2–83
China
  ancient area number T.2–31
  history to 420 A.D. 931 (930)
  modern area number T.2–51
China (Ceramics)
  art 738 (730)
  technology 666 (660)
Chinese language 495.1
    (400 / 495.1)
Chivalry (Custom) 394 (390)
Choral music 782.5 (782)
Chordates 596 (591/596)
Christian life 248 (230)
Christian Science 289.5
    (280 / 289.5)
Christianity 230
Christmas music 782.32 (782)
  religious observance 264 (230)
  social customs 394 (390)
Christology 232 (230)
Chronology
  astronomy 529 (520)
  history 902 (900)
Church architecture 726 (720)
Church furnishings
  Christianity 247 (230)
  other religions 290
Church government
  Christianity 262 (230)
  other religions 290
Church music 781.6 (781)
Church of Christ Scientist 289.5
    (280 / 289.5)
Church of England 283 (280 / 283)
Churches (Buildings) 726 (720)
Cigarette habit 613. 8 (613)
Cinema
  entertainment 791.43 (791)
Cinematography 778.5 (770)
Ciphers 652 (650)
Circulatory organs
  diseases 616.4 (610)
  physiology 612.1 (612)

Circuses 791.3 (791)
Ciskei (South Africa) T.2–6879
Cities and towns T.2–1732
  sociology 307.76 (307)
Citizenship 323 (320)
City planning 711 (710)
Civic art 710
Civics 323 (320)
Civil engineering 624
Civil law 346 (340)
Civil rights 323.4 (320)
Civil service 351 (350)
Civilization 909 (900)
Clairvoyance 133.8 (130)
Clarinet (Music) 788 (784 / 788)
Classes, Social 305.5 (305)
Classical (Greek and Roman)
  religion 292 (290/292)
Classical languages 480 (400 / 480)
Classical music 781.68 (781)
Cleaning
  home economics 648
  technology 667 (660)
Cleanliness, Personal 613.4 (613)
Clergy
  Christianity 253 (230)
Cleveland (England) T.2–428
Climate 551.6
Clinical psychology 616.89 (610)
Clocks 681
Clothing
  choice (Home econ.) 646.3 (646.2)
  construction
    home economics 646.4 (646.2)
    industry 687 (680)
  customs 391 (390)
Clubs 366
  special subjects T.1–06
Clywd (Wales) T.2–4291
Coaching 798.4 (796)
Coal 553 (550)
Coal industry 338.2 (338)
Coal mining 622
Coins
  economics 332.4 (332)
  numismatics 737 (730)
Coleraine (N. Ireland) T.2–4162
Collecting (Activity) 790.132
    (790.1)
Collections
  general 080
  literature 808 (800)
  specific lits. T.3–08
Collective bargaining 331.8 (331)
Collectivism
  economics 330.1 (330)
  political science 320
College life 378 (370)

142

Colombia	T.2–861
Colonies	325 (320)
Colonisation	325 (320)
Colorado (U.S.A.)	T.2–78
Colour	
physics	535.6 (535)
technology	667 (660)
Combat	355.4 (355)
Combat sports	796.8
	(796 / 796.8)
Comedy	T.3–2
theatre	792.2 (792)
Comets	523.6 (520)
Comics (Cartoons)	741.5 (740)
Commentaries	
(Bible)	220.7 (220)
Commerce	380.1
Commercial art	741.6 (740)
Commercial catalogues	T.2–029
Commonwealth of	
Nations	T.2–171241
Communicable	
diseases	616.9 (610)
Communication	001
engineering	621.38
office work	651.7 (651)
sociology	302.2 (302)
Communication	
satellites	
communication	384.5 (384)
engineering	629.4
Communications	380.3
Communism	
economics	330.1 (330)
political sci.	320
Community	307
Commuter traffic	388.4
Composite materials	
art	745.59
	(745 / 745.59)
Composition (Language)	808
Composition (Music)	781.3 (781)
Computer games	794.8
	(793 / 794.8)
Computers	004
engineering	621.39
programming	005 (004)
Conciliation (Labour)	331.8 (331)
Concrete	666 (660)
Concubinage	
customs	392 (390)
sociology	306.7 (306)
Conduct	
Christian ethics	241 (230)
customs	390
ethics	170
etiquette	395
Conducting (Music)	781.4 (781)

Conductivity	
electricity	
physics	537.6 (537)
Confessions of faith	
Christianity	238 (230)
other religions	290
Confirmation (Christian)	265 (230)
Conflict resolution	303.6 (303)
Conflict, Social	303.6 (303)
Confucianism	
philosophy	181 (100)
religion	299 (290 / 299)
Congo Republic	T.2–67
Congregational churches	285 (280 / 285)
Connacht (Republic of	
Ireland)	T.2–4171
Connecticut (U.S.A.)	T.2–74
Consciousness	153 (150)
Conservation	
animals	590.7
antiques	745.1
	(745 / 745.1)
art objects	702 (700)
biological resources	639.9 (639)
birds	598.07
	(591/598.07)
environment	574.07
paintings	751.6 (750)
plants	580.7
Constitutions	
law	342 (340)
political science	321 (320)
Construction (Buildings)	690
Consumer education	640
Contagious diseases	616.9 (610)
Contraception	613.9 (613)
Controversial knowledge	001.9 (001)
Convent life	255 (230)
Cooking	641.5
Cookstown (N. Ireland)	T.2–4162
Co-operation	
government	350
social welfare	361.7 (361)
Coptic languages	493 (400 / 493)
Coptic religion	281 (280 / 281)
Copyright	346 (340)
Coraciiformes	598.8
	(591/598.8)
Cornets (Music)	788 (784)
Cornish language	491.67
	(400/491.67)
Cornwall (England)	T.2–423
Corporations	658.11 (658)
Cosmetics	
chemical technology	668 (660)
customs	391 (390)
personal appearance	646.71 (646.7)
Cosmic rays	539.7 (539)

Cosmology
   astronomy — 523.1 (520)
   philosophy — 113 (100)
Costa Rica — T.2–7286
Costume *See* Clothing
Counselling
   education — 371.4
Counterfeit money — 332.4 (332)
Counter-Reformation
   (Christian) — 270 (230)
   European history — 940.23 (940)
Counting — 513
Country life — 307.72 (307)
Courts — 347 (340)
Courts and courtiers — 390
Courtship
   customs — 392 (390)
   sociology — 306.7 (306)
Crafts
   arts — 745.5
        (745 / 745.5)
Craigavon
   (N. Ireland) — T.2–4166
Creation
   artistic — 701 (800)
   Christian belief — 233 (230)
   literary — 801 (800)
   philosophy — 111 (100)
Creative ability — 700.19 (700)
Credit — 332.7 (332)
Credit cards — 332.7 (332)
Creeds
   Christianity — 238 (230)
   other religions — 290
Cricket (Game) — 796.358
        (796 / 796.358)
Crime
   control of — 364
   detection — 363.2
   law — 345 (340)
Crime victims
   social welfare — 362.8 (362)
Criminal law — 345 (340)
Criminal procedure — 345 (340)
Criminology — 364
Crippled persons
   medicine — 616 (610)
   social welfare — 362.4 (362)
Crocodiles — 597.9
        (591 / 597.9)
Crocheting — 746.43 (746)
Crops — 633–635 (630)
Crossword puzzles — 793.7
        (793 / 793.7)
Croquet — 736.354
        (796 / 796.354)
Crowd psychology — 302.3 (302)

Cruelty to animals
   ethics — 179 (170)
Crusades — 940.1 (940)
Crustaceans
   animal husbandry — 639.4 (639)
   zoology — 594 (591 / 594)
Cryotechnology — 621.5
Cryptogamia — 586 (580 / 586)
Cryptography — 652 (651)
Crystallography — 548 (540)
Cuba — T.2–7291
Cuckoos — 598.7
        (591 / 598.7)
Cultivating
   technology — 631.5 (630)
Cultivation of crops — 631.5 (630)
Cults
   Christian — 289.9
        (280 / 289.9)
   other religions — 290
Cultural transmision — 306.4 (306)
Culture (Sociology) — 306
Cumbria (England) — T.2–427
Curacao — T.2–7298
Currency (Money) — 332.4 (332)
Curriculums — 375 (370)
Customs (Social) — 390
Cybernetics — 004
Cymbals — 786.8
        (784 / 786.8)
Cymric language — 491.66
        (400 / 491.66)
Cycling
   sports — 796.6
        (796 / 796.6)
   transport — 388.3 (388)
Cyprus — T.2–564
Cytology — 574.8 (574)
   animal — 591.8 (591)
   human — 611 (610)
   plant — 581.8 (580)
Czech language — 491.8
        (400 / 491.8)
Czechoslovakia — T.2–437

D

Dadra (India) — T.2–547
Dahomey — T.2–66
Dairy technology — 637
Daman (India) — T.2–547
Dams — 627
Dance
   ballet — 792.8 (792)
   music — 781.5 (781)
   recreation — 793.3
        (793 / 793.3)
   theatre — 792.8 (792)

Dangers *See* Safety
Danish language 439.8
    (400 / 439.8)
Dard languages 491.49
    (400 / 491.49)
Darts (Game) 794.3
    (793 / 794.3)
Data bases 004
Data processing 004
  specific subjects T.1–028
Dating (Courtship)
  customs 392 (390)
  personal living 646.76 (646.7)
  sociology 306.7 (306)
Daydreaming 154 (150)
Dead, Disposal of
  customs 392 (390)
  social problems 363.7
Dead Sea Scrolls 229.8
Deaf-blindness
  medical aspects 617.7 (610)
  social welfare 362.41 (362)
Deaf-mute languages 419 (400)
Deafness
  medical aspects 617.8 (610)
  social welfare 362.42 (362)
Death customs 392 (390)
Death penalty
  criminology 364
  ethics 179 (170)
Debating 808.53 (808)
Decorations (House) 643.3 (643)
Decorations (Honours) 929.8 (929)
Decorative arts 745
Deep freezing food
  food technology 664 (660)
  home economics 641.4 (641)
Deer 599.73
  (591/599.73)
Defectives (Mental)
  social welfare 362.3 (362)
Defence, Military 355.4 (355)
Deflation (Economics) 332
Dehydrating food
  food technology 664 (660)
  home economics 641.4 (641)
Deities 210 (200)
  Christian 231 (230)
  other religions 290
Delaware (U.S.A.) T.2–75
Delinquency *See* Crime
Democracy 321 (320)
Demography 304.6 (304)
Demonology 133.4 (130)
Dendrology
  botany 582.16
  (581/582.16)
  forestry 634.9

Denmark T.2–489
Denominations, Religious
  Christianity 280
  other religions 290
Dental diseases 617.6 (610)
Dentistry 617.6 (610)
Department stores 658.8
Dependent states 321 (320)
Depth psychology 154 (150)
Depressions
  (Geological) T.2–144
Derbyshire (England) T.2–425
Derivations (Words) 412 (400)
  specific languages T.4–2
Dermatology 616.5 (610)
Derry (N. Ireland) T.2–4162
Desert regions T.2–154
Design, Industrial 745.2
  (745/745.2)
Destiny
  philosophy 122 (120)
Destitute persons 362.5 (362)
Detection (Criminal
  investigation) 363.2
Detention homes 365 (364)
Determinism 122 (120)
Developing countries T.2–172
Development (Biology)
  See Maturation
Development (Psychology) 155 (150)
Deviation (Social) 302.5 (302)
Devils
  Christianity 235 (230)
  occultism 133.4 (130)
Devonshire (England) T.2–423
Devotional literature
  Christian 242
  other religions 290
Dialectical materialism
  philosophy 100
  political ideology 320.1 (320)
Dialects 417 (400)
  specific languages T.4–7
Diaries 920
  specific subjects T.2–092
Dice games 795 (793 / 795)
Dicotyledons 583 (580 / 583)
Dictatorship 321 (320)
Dictionaries
  specific languages T.4–3
  other subjects T.4–03
  place names 910.3
  polyglot 413 (400)
Diesel engines 621.4
Diet (Food)
  home economics 641
  personal health 613.2 (613)
Dietetics 613.2 (613)

Digestive system (Human)
  diseases 616.3 (610)
  physiology 612 (612)
Digital computers 004
  engineering 621.39
  programming 005 (004)
Dinosaurs 567 (560)
Diplomacy 327 (320)
  customs 395
Directories T.2–025
Disablement
  medical aspects 616 (610)
  social welfare 362.1 (362)
Disarmament
  ethics 172 (170)
  law 341.2 (340)
  political science 327 (320)
Disasters
  history 904
  social action 363.3
Disciples of Christ
  Church 286 (280 / 286)
Discovery and exploration 910.9 (910)
Discriminatory
  practices
  ethics 177 (170)
  political science 323.4 (320)
Diseases and injuries
  animals
    veterinary science 636.089 (636)
    zoology 591.1 (591)
  humans 616 (610)
  plants
    agriculture 632 (630)
    botany 581.1 (580)
    public health 614.4 (614)
Displaced persons 325 (320)
Distributive trades 658.8
Diu (India) T.2–547
Divinatory arts 133.3 (130)
Diving
  sport 797.2
    (796 / 797.2)
  underwater exploration 622
Divinities 210 (200)
  Christian 231 (230)
  other religions 290
Divorce See Marriage
Djibouti T.2–67
Docks (Port facilities) 627
Doctrine (Theology)
  Christianity 230
  other religions 290
Dogs
  animal husbandry 636.7
    (636/636.7)
  racing 798.8
    (796/796.8)

  zoology 599.74
    (591 / 599.74)
Dolls 745.59
    (745 / 745.59)
Dolphins 599.5
    (591 / 599.5)
Domestic animals
  animal husbandry 636
  pets 636.088 (636)
  zoology 591.6 (591)
Domestic life
  customs 392 (390)
  home economics 646.7
Domestic safety 363.13 (363.1)
Domestic science 640
Domestic trade 381 (380.1)
Dominica T.2–7298
Dominican
  Republic T.2–7293
Dominoes (Game) 795.1
    (793 / 795.1)
Donegal (Republic
  of Ireland) T.2–4169
Donkeys
  animal husbandry 636.1 (636)
  zoology 599.725
    (591 / 599.725)
Dorset (England) T.2–423
Doves 598.6
    (591/598.6)
Down (Ireland) T.2–4165
Dowsing 133.3 (130)
Draft animals
  animal husbandry 636.08 (636)
  zoology 591.6 (591)
Drafting (Drawing) 604.2 (604)
Dragons (Folk
  literature) 398.24 (398)
Drama
  collections 808.82 (808)
  composition 808.2 (808)
  criticism 809.2 (809)
  specific literatures T.3–2
  theatre 792.1 (791)
Dramatic music 781.5 (781)
Draughts 794.22
    (793 / 794.22)
Dravidian languages 494 (490 / 494)
Drawing (Art) 741 (740)
Drawing, Technical 604.2 (604)
Dreams 154 (150)
Dresses See Clothing
Dressmaking
  home economics 646.4 (646.2)
  industry 687 (680)
Drinks
  home economics 641.2 (641)
  technology 663 (660)

Driving (Motor vehicles)
  regulations   343 (340)
  sport   796.7
                       (796/796.7)
  transport   388.3 (388)
Drug addictions
  ethics   178 (170)
  medicine   613.8 (610)
  social welfare   362.29 (362)
Drug therapies   615.5 (610)
Drug traffic control   363.4
Drums (Musical instrument)
  music   786.9
                     (784/786.9)
Drunkenness *See* Alcohol
  addiction
Drying food
  food technology   664 (660)
  home economics 641.4 (641)
Drypoint   767 (760)
Dublin (Republic
  of Ireland)   T.2–4183
Ducks
  animal husbandry 636.5 (636)
  zoology   598.3
                   (591/598.3)
Duplicating machines
  office management 652 (651)
Duplication (Documents) 652 (651)
Dumfries and Galloway
  (Scotland)   T.2–414
Dungannon (N. Ireland) T.2–4162
Durham (England)   T.2–428
Dutch Guiana   T.2–883
Dutch language   439.31
                (400/439.31)
Dwellings (Buildings)
  architecture   728
Dyeing
  art   746.6 (746)
  technology   667 (660)
Dyfed (Wales)   T.2–4292
Dyslexia
  medicine   616.8 (610)
  psychology   157 (150)

E

EDP   004
EEC   341.242 (340)
Ears
  diseases and injuries 617.8 (610)
  physiology   612.85 (612)
Earth
  astronomy   525 (520)
  geology   551
Earth sciences   550
Earthquakes   551.2 (551)
East Africa   T.2–676

East Anglia (England) T.2–426
East Indo-European
  languages   491 (400/491)
East Slavic languages 491.7
                (400/491.7)
East Sussex (England) T.2–422
Easter   263 (230)
Easter music   781.727 (781)
Eastern bloc
  (Political grouping) T.2–1717
Eastern Hemisphere T.2–1811
Eastern Orthodox
  Church   281.9
                (280/281.9)
Eating
  etiquette   395
  See also Food and drink
Ecclesiology (Christian) 262 (230)
Ecology   574.5
  animals   591.5 (591)
  humans   304.2 (304)
  plants   581.5 (580)
Economic biology 574.6 (574)
Economic botany 581.6 (580)
Economic geology 553 (550)
Economic zoology 591.6 (591)
Economics   330
Ecuador   T.2–866
Ecumenicalism   262 (230)
Edible animals
  animal husbandry 636
  zoology   591.6 (591)
Edible plants
  agriculture   633–635
  economic botany 581.6 (580)
Edinburgh (Scotland) T.2–4134
Education   370
  law   344
  religion (Christian) 268 (230)
  other religions   290
  other subjects   T.2–07
Education, Higher 378 (370)
Educational buildings
  architecture   727 (720)
Educational psychology 370.1 (370)
Educational sociology 370.1 (370)
Egg production   637
Egypt
  ancient area number T.2–32
  modern area number T.2–62
  history to 640 A.D. 932 (930/932)
  history from 640 A.D. 962 (960)
Eire   T.2–417
El Salvador   T.2–7284
Elastomers   678 (670/678)
Elderly persons
  medicine   618.92 (610)
  psychology   155 (150)

Elderly persons (*continued*)

social welfare	362.6 (362)
sociology	305.2 (305)
Electoral systems	324 (320)

Electric apparatus
and circuits

power generation	621.3
electronic eng.	621.38
Electric power	621.3

Electrical currents

physics	537.6 (537)

Electrical appliances

manufacture	683 (680)
Electrical engineering	621.3

Electrical heating

buildings	697 (690)
Electrical lighting	697 (690)
Electrical measurements	621.37 (621.3)
Electrical testing	621.37 (621.3)
Electrical work	696 (690)

Electricity

physics	537

*See also entries beginning
with* Electro *and*
Electrical

Electro-magnetic engineering	621.3
Electronic apparatus and	621.38
circuits	
Electronic data processing	004
Electronic games	794.8
	(793 / 794.8)
Electronic music	786.7
	(784 / 786.7)

Electronics

engineering	621.38
physics	537.5 (537)

*See also entries beginning
with* Electronic

Electrophonic music	786 (784/786)
Electrostatics	537.2 (537)
Elephants	599.6
	(591 / 599.6)

Elevations (Physio-

graphic)	T.2–143
Elizabethan literature	T.3P(England)
Elocution	808.5 (808)
Emancipation of slaves	326 (320)
Emblems, National	929.9 (929)
Embroidery	746.44 (746)
Emergency aid	363.3
Emigration	325 (320)

Emotionally disturbed
persons

medical aspects	616.89 (610)
social welfare	362.2
Emotions	152 (150)

Employee-employer

relations	331.8 (331)

Employment	331

Enamelling

handicraft	738 (730)
Encyclopaedias	030
place names	910.03 (910)
other subjects	T.3–03

Endocrine system

diseases and injuries	616.4 (610)
physiology	612

Energy

economics	333.7 (333)
technology	621.4 (621.4)
Engineering	620
Engineering materials	620.1

England

ancient area number	T.2–361
modern area number	T.2–42
history to 500 A.D.	936.1
history from 500 A.D.	942

See also British Isles,
United Kingdom

English drama	882
English essays	824
English fiction	823
English humour	827
English letters	
(Belles-lettres)	826
English literature	820
English novels	823
English poetry	821
English prose	828
English short stories	823
Engraving, Metal	765 (760)
Entertainers	791.092 (791)
Entertainments	790
Entomology	595.7
	(591 / 595.7)

Environment,

Conservation of	575.07

Environmental engineering

municipal structures	628
human environment	620.8 (620)
Environmental protection	363.7

Epidemics

medical history	616.9 (610)
social welfare	362.1 (362)
Epidemiology	616.9 (610)
social welfare	362.1 (362)
Epidemiology	616.9 (610)
Epilepsy	616.8 (610)

Episcopacy

Christian church govt.	262 (230)
Epistemology	120 (100)
Epistles (New Testament)	227 (225)

Equal opportunity

civil rights	323.4 (320)
Equatorial Guinea	T.2–67
Equestrian sports	798 (796 / 798)

148

Equidae	599.725	Exchanges, Stock and	
	(591 / 599.725)	commodity	332.6 (332)
See also Horses		Excretion	612.4 (612)
Ergonomics	620.8 (620)	Executive branch of	
Erosion (Geology)	551.3 (551)	government	350
Erse language	491.63	Executive management	658
	(400 / 491.63)	Exegesis (Bible)	220.6 (220)
Eschatology		Exercise	613.7 (613)
Christian	236 (230)	Exhibitions	T.1–074
Eskimo-Aleut languages	497 (400 / 497)	Expenditure	
Espionage	327 (320)	business	658.1 (658)
Esperanto language	499.9	home economics	640
	(400 / 499.9)	Experimental medicine	619 (610)
Essays (Belles-lettres)		Exploration and discovery	910.9 (910)
collections	808.84 (800)	Explosives	662 (660)
composition	808.4 (800)	Exporting and importing	382 (380.1)
criticism	809.4 (800)	Expression (Speaking)	808.5 (808)
specific literatures	T.3–4	External affairs	327 (320)
Essex (England)	T.2–426	Extinct animals	591.04 (591)
Estonian language	494 (400 / 494)	Extinct birds	598.04
Estuaries	T.2–169		(591 / 598.04)
Etching	767 (760)	Extraction industries	
Ethics	170	economics	338.2 (338)
Christianity	241 (240)	technology	622
Evangelism (Christianity)		Extrasensory perception	133.8 (130)
pastoral work	253 (230)	Extraterrestrial worlds	T.2–99
Ethiopia	T.2–63	*See also* Space	
Ethnic groups		Eyes	
social welfare	362.8 (362)	diseases and injuries	617.7 (610)
sociology	305.7 (305)	social welfare	362.42 (362)
Ethnology		physiology	612.84 (612)
biology	572 (570)		
sociology	306	**F**	
Etiquette	395		
Etruscan sculpture	733 (730)	Fabric furnishings	
Etymology	412 (400)	home economics	643.3 (643)
specific languages	T.4–2	manufacture	684.3 (680)
Europe		Fabric painting	
ancient area number	T.2–36	art	746.9 (746)
modern area number	T.2–4	Factories	
history to 500 A.D.	936 (930 / 936)	management	658.2 (658)
history from 500 A.D.	940	Faeroes Islands	T.2–491
regional organizations	341.242 (340)	Faeroese language	439 (400 / 439)
European Economic		Fairy tales	398.21 (398.2)
Community	341.242 (340)	Faith	200
Euthanasia	179 (170)	*See also entries*	
Evangelical churches		*beginning with*	
Lutheran Church	284 (280 / 284)	Religion *and* Religious	
See also other specific		Faith healing	
evangelical churches		medicine	615.8 (610)
Evangelism (Christianity)		Falconiformes	598.9
pastoral work	253 (230)		(591 / 598.9)
spiritual renewal	269 (230)	Falconry	799.2
Evolution, Organic	575 (570)		(796 / 799.2)
Ex-service personnel		Falcons	
social welfare	362.8 (362)	sports	799.2 (796)
Examinations	371.3	zoology	598.9
Exchange (Money)	332.4 (332)		(591 / 598.9)

Falkland Islands	T.2–971	Feudalism	
Families		European history	940.1 (940)
ethics	173 (170)	political science	321 (320)
family histories	929.1 (929)	Fibre products	677 (670)
family life (Home econ.)	646.7	Fiction	
law	346 (340)	collections	808.83 (800)
social welfare	362.8 (362)	composition	808.3 (800)
sociology	306.8	criticism	809.3 (800)
Family law	346 (340)	specific literatures	T.3–3
Family living	646	Field athletics	796.42
Fancy work (Handicrafts)	746.4 (746)		(796/796.42)
Far East	T.2–5	Field crops	633
regional organizations	341.247 (340)	Field hockey	796.355
Farm buildings	631.2 (630)		(796/796.355)
Farm equipment	631.2 (630)	Field sports	796
Farming	630	Field study (Nature)	574.07
Farsi language	491.5	animals	590.7
	(400/491.5)	birds	598.07
Fascism	320	plants	580.7
Fashion		Fife (Scotland)	T.2–412
clothing	646.3 (646.2)	Fighter planes	
customs	391 (390)	military science	358 (355)
design	746	technology	623
Fasts and feasts		Figurines	738 (730)
Christianity	263 (230)	Fiji	T.2–96
other religions	290	Filing (Documents)	
Feasts and fasts		library science	025 (020)
Christianity	263 (230)	office work	651.5 (651)
other religions	290	Financial economics	332
Federal governments		Financial management	
administration	351 (350)	business	658.15 (658)
Feelings (Emotions)	152 (150)	home economics	640
Feet		Fine arts	700
diseases and injuries	617 (610)	Finland	T.2–4897
Felidae	599.75	Finnish language	494 (400/494)
	(591/599.75)	Fire fighting	363.37 (363.3)
See also Cats		Fire safety	
Felonies *See* Crime		social services	363.37 (363.3)
Females (Human)		technology	628
diseases	618.1 (610)	Firearms	
other aspects *see* Women		art metalwork	739.7 (730)
Feminism	305.3 (305)	manufacture	683.4 (680)
Fencing (Swordplay)	796.8	ordnance	355.4 (355)
	(796/796.8)	Fireworks	
Fermanagh (N. Ireland)	T.2–4162	chemical technology	662 (660)
Ferns	587 (580/587)	displays	791
Ferrous metals		First aid	616.02 (610)
manufacture	672 (670)	Fishes	
metallurgy	669	paleozoology	567 (560)
Ferry transportation	386	zoology	597.3
Fertilizers			(591/597.3)
agriculture	631 (630)	*See also* Fishing	
technology	668 (660)	Fishing	
Ferungulata	599.7	animal husbandry	639.2 (639)
	(591/599.7)	sport	799.1
Festivals (Religion)			(796/799.1)
Christianity	263 (230)	Fission plants (Botany)	589.9
other religions	290		(581/589.9)

Flags (Insignia)	929.9 (929)	Forensic medicine	614.1 (614)
Flags (Non-verbal		Forest fires	634.9
communication)	001	Forest regions	T.2–152
Flemish language	439.31	Forestry	634.9
	(400.439.31)	Formosa	T.2–51
Flemish painting	759.92 (750)	Fortified buildings	
Flight	629.1	architecture	725
Floor coverings		military science	355.4 (355)
building	690	Fortunetelling	133.3 (130)
home economics	643.3 (643)	Fossils	560
Floral arts	745.9	Found objects	745.58
	(745 / 745.9)	Foundations	
Florida (U.S.A.)	T.2–75	building	690
Flowers		civil engineering	624.1 (624)
arrangement	745.9	Foundry practice	671 (670)
	(745 / 745.9)	France	
growing	635.9	ancient area number	T.2–36
Fluids, Mechanics of	532 (531)	modern area number	T.2–44
Flute	788 (784)	history to 500 A.D.	936 (930 / 936)
Flying (Sport)	797.5	history from 500 A.D.	944
	(796 / 797.5)	painters	759.4 (750)
Folk arts	745	philosophers	194 (100)
Folk literature	398.2	Franco, Francisco (Spain)	946.081 (946)
Folk lore	398.2	Free enterprise	330.1 (330)
Folk medicine	615.8 (610)	Freedom of assembly	323.4
Folk music	781.62 (781)	Freedom of conscience	323.4 (320)
Folk songs	782.42 (782)	Freedom of speech	323.4 (320)
Folklore	398.2	Freedom of the press	323.4 (320)
Food and drink		Freezing (Food	
customs	392 (390)	preparation)	
home economics	641	food technology	664 (660)
manufacture	664 (660)	home economics	641.4 (641)
nutrition	613.2 (613)	French Congo	T.2–67
social welfare	363.8	French Guiana	T.2–882
Food animals		French language	440 (400 / 440)
animal husbandry	636	French literature	840
economic zoology	591.6 (591)	French Revolution	944.04 (944)
Food industry		Friends, Society of (Quakers)	289.6
economics	338.1 (338)		(280 / 289.6)
technology	664 (664)	Frigid zones	T.2–11
Food preservation	641.4 (641)	Frogs	
Food storage	641.4 (641)	zoology	597.6
Food supply	363.8		(591 / 597.6)
Football (American)	796.332	Fruit growing	634
	(796 / 796.332)	Fuels	
Football (Canadian)	796.335	chemical technology	662 (660)
	(796 / 796.335)	Fundamental education	372 (370)
Football (Rugby)	796.333	Funerals	
	(796 / 796.333)	customs	392 (390)
Football (Soccer)	796.334	Fungi	588 (580 / 588)
	(797 / 796.334)	Fur	
Forecasting	303.4 (303)	art	745.53
management	658		(745 / 745.53)
mathematics	519	manufacture	
weather	551.6	material	675 (670)
Foreign affairs	327 (320)	product	685 (680)
Foreign exchange	332.4 (332)	Fur (Material)	679 (670)
Foreign trade	382 (380.1)	Fur (Product)	685 (680)

151

Furniture
  antiques   745.1
                              (745 / 745.1)
  decorative arts   749 (745 / 749)
  home economics   643.3 (643)
  manufacture   684.1 (680)

G

Gabon   T.2–67
Gaelic language   491.62
                              (400 / 491.62)
Galaxies   523.1 (520)
Galleries (Art)   708 (700)
Galliformes   598.6
                              (591 / 598.6)
Galloway (Scotland) T.2–414
Gambia   T.2–665
Gambling
  ethics   175 (170)
  gaming   795 (793 / 795)
Game bird
  animal husbandry 636.6 (636)
  sport   799.2
                              (796 / 799.2)
Games   790
  folk literature   398.5
Games, Indoor   793
Games, Outdoor   796
Gamma rays   539.7 (539)
Gangs   302.3 (302)
Gaols   365 (364)
Garbage disposal   363.72 (363.7)
Garden crops   635
Gardening   635
Garments *See* Clothing
Gas
  chemical technology 664 (660)
  chemistry   543 (540)
  heating (Buildings) 697 (690)
  lighting (Buildings) 697 (690)
  mechanics   533 (530)
  supply (Buildings) 697 (690)
Gas turbines   621.4
Gastric diseases   616.3 (610)
Gazankulu(South Africa) T.2–6829
Gazetteers   910.3
  specific places   T.1–03
Gems
  economic geology 553 (550)
  jewelry   745.594
                         (745 / 745.594)
Genealogy   929.1 (929)
Generation gap   305.2 (305)
Genetic psychology 155 (150)
Genetics   575.1 (574)
  animals   591.1 (591)
  humans   573
  plants   581.1 (580)

Genito-urinary system
  diseases and injuries 616.6
                          (610 / 616.6)
  physiology   612.4 (612)
Gentry
  genealogy   929.7 (929)
Geodesy   526 (520)
Geodetic surveying 526.9 (520)
Geography   910
  specific subjects   T.1–091–099
Geology   551
Geometry   516
Geophysics   551
Georgia (U.S.A.)   T.2–75
Geriatrics   618.97 (610)
German Democratic
    Republic
  area number   T.2–431
  history   943.1 (943)
German language   430 (400 / 430)
German literature   830
Germanic languages 430 (400 / 430)
Germanic religions 293 (290 / 293)
Germany
  ancient area number T.2–363
  modern area number T.2–43
  history to 480 A.D. 963.3
                         (930 / 936.3)
  history from 480 A.D. 943
  painters   759.3 (750)
  philosophers   193 (100)
Germany, Federal Republic
  See Germany
Gesture (speaking)   808.5 (808)
Ghana   T.2–667
Ghettoes   307.76 (307)
Ghosts
  folk stories   398.25 (398.2)
  occultism   133.1 (130)
Gifted children
  education   371.9 (370)
Giraffes   599.73
                       (591/599.73)
Girl guides   366
Girl scouts   366
Glaciers   551.3 (551)
Glaciology   551.3 (551)
Glandular system
  diseases and injuries 616.4 (610)
  physiology   612
Glamorgan (Wales) T.2–4292
Glass
  ceramic arts   738 (730)
  decorative arts   748 (745 / 748)
  technology   666 (660)
Gliding (Air sport) 797.5
                       (796 / 797.5)
Glossaries   T.1–03

Gloucestershire
(England)   T.2–424
Glues   668 (660)
Gluttony   178 (170)
Gnosticism   210 (200)
Goa (India)   T.2–547
Goats
  animal husbandry   636.3 (636)
  zoology   599.73
                        (591/599.73)
God
  Christianity   231 (230)
Gods
  religion   210 (200)
Goldsmithing
  art metalwork   739.2 (730)
Golf   796.352
                        (796/796.352)
Good and evil
  philosophy   111 (100)
  religion (Christian) 231 (230)
  other religions   290
Gorillas   599.8
                        (591/599.8)
Gospels (New Testament) 226 (225)
Gossip   177 (170)
Gothic architecture   723 (720)
Gothic painting   759.02 (750)
Gothic Revival architecture 742.2 (720)
Government administration 351–354 (350)
Grace and salvation
  Christianity   234 (230)
  other religions   290
Grains
  agriculture   633 (630)
Grammar   415 (400)
  specific languages T.4–5
Grampian Mts.
  (Scotland)   T.2–412
Graphic arts   760
Graphic design   741.6 (740)
Graphology   137 (130)
Grasslands   T.2–145
Gravity   531
Great Britain See British Isles,
  United Kingdom
Greece
  ancient area number T.2–38
  modern area number   T.2–495
  history to 323 A.D.   938 (930/938)
  history from 323 A.D. 949.5 (949)
Greek islands   T.2–499
Greek language
  ancient   480 (400/480)
  modern   489 (400/489)
Greek literature
  ancient   880 (800/880)
  modern   889 (800/889)

Greek Orthodox Church   281.9
                        (280/281.9)
Greek philosophy
  ancient   182
Greek religion
  ancient   292 (290/292)
Greek sculpture   733 (730)
Greenland   T.2–98
Greeting cards
  handicrafts   745.594
                        (745/745.594)
Grenada   T.2–7298
Grooming, Personal   646.71 (646.7)
Ground transportation   388
Ground warfare   356 (355)
Group sociology   302.3 (302)
Growth   574.1
  animals   591.3 (591)
  humans   612.6 (612)
  plants   581.3 (580)
Guadeloupe   T.2–7297
Guatemala   T.2–7281
Guianas (South
  America)   T.2–88
Guidance and counselling
  education   371.4
Guide books
  world travel   910.2
  See also the geography of
    specific places
Guided missiles
  military science   355.4 (355)
  technology   623.4 (623)
Guilds (Trade unions)   331.88 (331)
Guinea, Equatorial T.2–67
Guinea, Gulf of
  (Islands)   T.2–66
Guinea-Bissau   T.2–66
Guinea Republic   T.2–66
Guitars
  music   787.8
                        (784/878.8)
Gujarat (India)   T.2–547
Gujarati language   491.47
                        (400/491.47)
Gulls   598.3
                        (591/598.3)
Guns
  arms and armour   739.7 (730)
  ordnance
    military science   355.4 (355)
    technology
      military hardware 623.4 (623)
      small firearms   683.4 (683)
Guyana   T.2–881
Guyane   T.2–882
Gwent (Wales)   T.2–4292
Gwynedd (Wales)   T.2–4291

Gymnastics		technology	604.7	
sports	796.4	Health		
	(796/796.4)	medicine	610	
therapeutics	615.8 (610)	social welfare	362.1 (362)	
Gymnosperms	585 (580/585)	Hearing		
Gynaecology	618.1 (610)	diseases and injuries	617.8 (610)	
Gypsy language	491.49	physiology	612.85 (612)	
	(400/491.49)	Heart		
		pathology	616.1 (610)	
H		physiology	612	
Habitats (Biology)	574.909 (574)	Heat		
animals	591.9 (591)	building technology	697 (690)	
birds	598.09	physics	536	
plants	581.9 (580)	technology	621.4	
Hair		Heat transfer	536	
diseases and injuries	616.5 (610)	Heather	583 (581/583)	
personal appearance	646.71 (646.7)	Hebrew language	492.7	
physiology	612.7 (612)		(400/492.7)	
Haiti	T.2–7294	Helicopters		
Hamitic languages	493 (400/493)	technology	629.1	
Hamito-Semitic languages	492 (400/492)	transportation	387.73 (387.7)	
Hampshire (England)	T.2–422	Hellenic languages	480 (400/480)	
Hand languages	419 (400)	Hellenistic		
Hand tools	621.9 (621.8)	*See* Greece, Greek		
Handball	796.32	Hemispheres (Geographical		
	(796/796.32)	areas)	T.2–181	
Handicapped persons		Heraldry	929.6 (929)	
medical aspects	616 (610)	design	745.6 (745)	
social welfare	362.1 (362)	Heredity		
Handicrafts		biology	575 (570)	
arts	745.5 (745)	sociology	304.5 (304)	
Handwriting		Hereford (England)	T.2–424	
calligraphy	745.6 (745)	Heresies		
language	411 (400)	Christianity	270	
Hang-gliding	797.5	other religions	290	
	(796/797.5)	Heroes (Folk literature)	398.22 (398)	
Hangings (Decorations)		Hertfordshire (England)	T.2–425	
home economics	643.3 (643)	Higher education	378 (370)	
interior decoration	746.3 (746)	Highlands (Scotland)	T.2–4111	
Hapsburg dynasty		Highways		
Spanish history	946.05 (946)	engineering	625.7	
Harbours		safety	363.125	
engineering	627	transportation	388.1 (388)	
transportation	387.1 (387)	Hills (Physiographic		
Hardware		feature)	T.2–143	
manufacture	683 (680)	Hindi language	491.43	
Harps			(400/491.43)	
music	787 (784/787)	Hinduism	294.5	
Harpsichords			(290/294.5)	
music	786 (784/786)	Histology	574.8 (574)	
Harvesters (Machines)	631.2 (630)	animal	591.8 (591)	
Harvesting	631.5 (630)	plant	581.8 (580)	
Hatcheries (Fish)	639.3 (639)	Historical geography	911 (910)	
Hausa language	493 (400/493)	History	909	
Hawaii (U.S.A.)	T.2–96	specific subjects	T.1–09	
Hazardous machinery	363.18 (363.1)	History, Ancient	930	
Hazardous materials		History, Modern	940–990	
safety	363.17	Hoaxes	001.9 (001)	

154

Hobbies	790.1 (790)	
Hockey, Field	796.355	
	(796 / 796.355)	
Hockey, Ice	796.9	
	(796 / 796.9)	
Holidays		
customs	394 (390)	
Christian	263 (230)	
other religions	290	
Holland	T.2–492	
Holography	621.36 (621.3)	
Holy Roman Empire	T.2–43	
history	943	
Home Counties		
(England)	T.2–422	
Home economics	640	
Home nursing	649.8 (649)	
Homeopathy	615.5 (610)	
Homicide		
criminology	364	
ethics	179 (170)	
law	345 (340)	
Hominidae	599.9(591/599.9)	
Homosexuality		
ethics	176 (170)	
sociology	306.7 (306)	
Honduras	T.2–7283	
Honey production	638	
Hong Kong	T.2–5125	
Hopscotch (Game)	796.1(796/796.1)	
Horology		
clock manufacture	681 (680)	
time measurement	529	
Horse racing	798.4	
	(796 / 798.4)	
Horses		
animal husbandry	636.1 (636)	
sport	798 (796 / 798)	
zoology	599.725	
	(591 / 599.725)	
Horticulture	635	
Hospitality	177 (170)	
Hospitals		
medical aspects	610	
social welfare	362.1 (362)	
Hotel management	647	
House furnishings	643.3 (643)	
House plants	635.9 (635)	
Household equipment		
home economics	643	
Household appliances		
home economics	643	
manufacture	683 (680)	
Household management	640	
Housekeeping	648	
Houses		
architecture	728	
building	690	

Housing		
home economics	643	
social welfare	363.5	
Human behaviour		
psychology	150	
sociology	301–307	
Human beings		
paleozoology	569 (560)	
zoology	599.9	
	(591 / 599.9)	
See also Anthropology,		
Civilization, Ecology,		
Ethnology, Psychology,		
Sociology		
Human ecology	304.2 (304)	
Human figure (Art)	757 (750)	
Human rights	323.4 (320)	
Humberside (England)	T.2–428	
Humour		
collections	808.87 (808)	
composition	808.7 (808)	
criticism	809.7 (809)	
specific literatures	T.3–7	
Hungarian language	494 (400 / 494)	
Hungary	T.2–439	
Hunt the thimble (Game)	793.2	
	(793/793.2)	
Hunting		
animal husbandry	639	
sports	799 (796 / 799)	
Hydraulic engineering	627	
Hydraulic power engineering	621.2	
Hydrographic biology	574.92 (574)	
Hydrology	551.4 (551)	
Hygiene	613	
Hymns		
Christian worship	242 (230)	
music	782.27 (782)	
Hypnotism		
psychology	154 (150)	
therapy	615.8 (610)	

I

Iberian peninsula		
ancient area number	T.2–366	
modern area number	T.2–46	
history to 500 A.D.	936.6	
	(930 / 936.6)	
history from 500 A.D.	946	
Ibo language	496 (400 / 496)	
Ice (Geology)	551.2 (551)	
Ice hockey	796.9	
	(796 / 796.9)	
Ice skating	796.9	
	(796/796.9)	
Ice sports	796.9	
	(796 / 796.9)	
Iceland	T.2–491	

Icelandic language	439 (400/439)	Industrial safety	363.11 (363.1)
Iconography	704 (700)	Industries	
Idaho (U.S.A.)	T.2–79	economics	338
Ideographs	411 (400)	management	658
Illinois (U.S.A.)	T.2–77	technology	600
Illness *See* Diseases and		Infants	
injuries		psychology	155 (150)
Illumination		sociology	305.2 (305)
decorative arts	745.6	Infectious diseases	616.9 (610)
	(745/745.6)	Inflation	332.4 (332)
lighting	697 (690)	Information	001
Illustrations		sociology	302.2 (302)
art	741.7 (740)	Information science	020
specific subjects	T.1–022	Infrared light	535.8 (535)
Imagination	153 (150)	Inheritance law	346 (340)
Immigration	325 (320)	Injuries *See* Diseases and	
Immortality		injuries	
Christian doctrine	234 (230)	Ink painting	751 (750)
philosophy	128 (100)	Inland waters	T.2–169
Imperialism	325 (320)	transportation	386
Imprisonment	365 (364)	Inorganic chemistry	546 (540)
Incas	985 (980)	Insanity	
Income, National	339 (330)	medical aspects	616.89 (610)
Income tax		social welfare	362.2 (362)
law	343 (340)	Insects	
public finance	336 (330)	animal husbandry	638
Incorporated companies	658.11 (658)	zoology	595.7
Incunabula	090 (010)		(591/595.7)
bibliography	011	Insignias	929
Indexes (Documentary)	011	Institutions (Social)	306
specific subjects	T.1–016	Instruction *See* Education	
Indexing (Library operation)	025 (020)	Instrumental music	784
India		Instruments	
ancient area number	T.2–34	manufacture	681 (680)
modern area number	T.2–54	Insurance	368 (360)
history to 647 A.D.	934 (930/934)	Intelligence (Espionage)	
history from 647 A.D.	954 (950)	international relations	327 (320)
Indian Ocean	T.2–165	international law	341 (340)
Indian Ocean region	T.2–1824	Intelligence (Psychology)	153 (150)
Indiana (U.S.A.)	T.2–77	Intelligence testing	153.9 (150)
Indic languages	491.4	Interdenominational activity	
	(400/491.4)	Christianity	262 (230)
Indic religions	294	Interior decoration	
Individualism		arts	747
social psychology	302.5	home economics	643.3 (643)
Indo-European languages	410 (400)	Interlingua (Language)	499.9
Indonesia	T.2–598		(400/499.9)
Indoor bowling	794.6	Internal combustion engines	629.2
	(793/794.6)	Internal commerce	382 (380.1)
Indoor games	793	International law	341 (340)
Industrial accidents	363.11 (363.1)	International Red Cross	361.7 (361)
Industrial art	745.2	International relations	327 (320)
	(745/745.2)	Interpersonal relations	158 (150)
Industrial design	745.2	Intertestamental works	
	(745/745.2)	(Bible)	229
Industrial hazards	363.11 (363.1)	Intestines	
Industrial relations	331.8 (331)	diseases and injuries	616.3 (610)
Industrial research	607	physiology	612

156

Inventions and		
patents	608	
Invertebrates	592 (591/592)	
Investment (Finance)	332.6 (332)	
Iowa (U.S.A.)	T.2–77	
Iran		
ancient area number	T.2–35	
modern area number	T.2–55	
history to 637 A.D.	935 (930/935)	
history from 637 A.D.	955 (950)	
Iranian languages	491.5	
	(400/491.5)	
Iraq		
ancient area number	T.2–35	
modern area number	T.2–35	
history to 637 A.D.	935	
history from 637 A.D.	995	
Ireland		
ancient area number	T.2–361	
modern area number	T.2–415	
history to 410 A.D.	936.1	
history from 410 A.D.	941.5	
Ireland, Republic of		
ancient area number	T.2–361	
modern area number	T.2–415	
history to 410 A.D.	936.1	
history from 410 A.D.	941.5	
See also British Isles		
Irish Gaelic language	491.62	
	(400/491.62)	
Iron and steel		
industry		
metallurgy	669	
technology	672 (670)	
Irrigation		
agriculture	631.7 (630)	
hydraulic engineering	627	
Islam	297 (290/297)	
Islamic art	709 (700)	
Islands (Physiographic		
feature)	T.2–142	
Isle of Man (British		
Isles)	T.2–427	
Isle of Wight (British		
Isles)	T.2–422	
Israel	T.2–5694	
Italian language	450 (400/450)	
Italian literature	850	
Italic languages	470 (400/470)	
Italy		
ancient area number	T.2–37	
modern area number	T.2–45	
history to 476 A.D.	937	
history from 476 A.D.	945	
painters	759.5 (750)	
philosophers	195 (100)	
Ivory carvings	736 (730)	
Ivory Coast	T.2–66	

J

Jails	365 (364)	
Jainism	294.4	
	(200/294.4)	
Jamaica	T.2–7292	
Jammu (India)	T.2–546	
Japan	T.2–52	
Japanese language	495.6	
	(400/495.6)	
Jazz music	781.76 (781)	
Jehovah's Witnesses	289.9	
	(280/289.9)	
Jellyfish	593 (591/593)	
Jersey (British Isles)	T.2–4234	
Jesus Christ	232 (230)	
Jewelry		
decorative arts	745.594	
	(745/745.594)	
Jews		
sociology	305.7 (305)	
See also Judaism		
Jordan	T.2–5695	
Journalism	070	
Journals (Publications)	050	
specific subjects	T.1–05	
Judaism	296 (290/296)	
Judo	796.8	
	(796/796.8)	
Juggling	793.8	
	(793/793.8)	
Jumping (Horse)	798 (796/798)	
Justice	340	
Juvenile delinquency	364	
Juveniles		
See headings beginning		
Child and		
Children		

K

Kampuchea	T.2–596	
Kangaroos		
animal husbandry	636.9	
	(636/636.9)	
zoology	599.1	
	(591/599.1)	
Kansas (U.S.A.)	T.2–78	
Karate	796.8	
	(796/796.8)	
Karnataka (India)	T.2–548	
Kashmir (India)	T.2–546	
Kashmiri language	491.49	
	(400/491.49)	
Kent (England)	T.2–422	
Kentucky (U.S.A.)	T.2–76	
Kenya	T.2–6762	
Keyboard instruments		
music	786 (784/786)	

Khmer Republic   T.2–596
Kingfishers   598.8
                              (591/598.8)
Kings and rulers   929.7 (929)
Kinship systems   306.8 (306)
Kites (Toy)   796.1
                              (796/796.1)
Knighthood
  customs   390
  genealogy   929.7 (929)
  history   940.1 (940)
Knights
  history   940.1 (940)
  military science   355.3 (355)
Knitting   746.43 (746)
Knowledge   001
  sociology   306.4 (306)
Koran   297.8
                              (290/297.8)
Korea   T.2–519
Kuwait   T.2–53
KwaZulu   T.2–6849

L

Laboratories
  chemistry   542 (540)
  other subjects   T.1–028
Labour   331
Labour economics   331
Labour force   331.1 (331)
Labour law   344 (340)
Labour management   658.3 (658)
Labour market   331.1 (331)
Labour relations   331.8 (331)
Labour unions   331.88 (331)
Labrador (Canada)   T.2–718
Lace
  handicrafts   746.2 (740)
Lacemaking   746.2 (746)
Lacrosse   796.347
                              (796/796.347)
Lake District
  (England)   T.2–427
Lakes (Physiographic
  feature)   T.2–169
Lakshadweep (India)   T.2–548
Lampshade making   745.593
                              (745/745.593)
Lancashire (England)   T.2–427
Land economics   333
Land forms
  (Physiographic
  feature)   T.2–14
Land warfare   356 (355)
Landscape design   712 (710)
Language   400
Language groups
  sociology   305.7 (305)

Language variety   417
  specific languages   T.4–7
Laos   T.2–594
Larks   598.8
                              (591/598.9)
Larne (N. Ireland)   T.2–4161
Las Palmas (Spain)   T.2–649
Lasers   621.36 (621.3)
Latex See Rubber
Latin America   T.2–8
Latin language   470 (400/470)
Latter Day Saints, Church of 289.3
                              (280/289.3)
Latvian language   491.9
                              (400/491.9)
Laundering
  home economics   648
  industry   667 (660)
Law   340
Lawn bowling   796.32
                              (796/796.32)
Lawn tennis   796.342
                              (796/796.342)
Leadership
  management   658
  political science   320
League of Nations   341.22 (340)
Learning
  psychology   370.1 (370)
  specific subjects   T.2–07
Leasing   331.1 (333)
Leather
  art   745.53
                              (745/745.53)
  technology   675 (670)
Leather (Product)
  manufacture   685 (680)
Lebanon   T.2–5692
Lebowa (South Africa)   T.2–6829
Lecturing   800
Leeches   595 (591/595)
Leeward Islands   T.2–7297
Legal procedures   347 (340)
Legends   398.2
Legislation   340
Legislative bodies   328 (320)
Leicestershire (England)   T.2–425
Leinster (Republic of
  Ireland)   T.2–418
Leisure
  ethics   175 (100)
Lent   263 (230)
Lesotho   T.2–6816
Letter writing
  business   652 (651)
  composition   800
Lettering   745.6
                              (745/745.6)

Letters (Correspondence)
  business   652 (651)
  composition   800
  specific literatures   T.3–6
Lexicography   413 (400)
Liberia   T.2–66
Liberty of the press   323.4 (320)
Librarianship   020
Libraries   027 (020)
Library catalogues   011
Library science   020
Libya   T.2–612
License plates   929.9 (929)
Liechtenstein   T.2–436
Life
  biology   577 (574)
  philosophy   128 (100)
Life sciences   570
Lifeboats
  public safety   363.123
Light
  physics   535
Lighthouses
  navigation   623.8
  transportation safety 363.123
  water transportation 387.1 (387)
Lighting   697 (690)
  electrical engineering 621.32 (621.3)
Limavady (N. Ireland) T.2–4162
Limited companies   658.11 (658)
Lincolnshire (England) T.2–425
Linguistics   410 (400)
Liquor problem   363.4
Lisburne (N. Ireland) T.2–4161
Literature (Belles-lettres) 800
Lithography   763 (760)
Liturgical music   781.6 (781)
Liturgy and ritual
  Christianity   264 (230)
  other religions   290
Livestock   636
Lizards   597.9
                    (591 / 597.9)
Lobsters
  animal husbandry   639.4
  zoology   594 (591/594)
Local government   352 (350)
Local transportation 388.4
Locksmithing   683.3 (680)
Locomotives
  engineering   625.1
Logic   160
Logic, Symbolic   511.3
London (England)   T.2–421
Londonderry (Ireland) T.2–4162
Lorries
  engineering   629.2
  transportation   388.3 (388)

Lothian (Scotland)   T.2–413
Louisiana (U.S.A.)   T.2–76
Love
  psychology   152 (150)
  sociology   306.7 (306)
Low Countries (Europe) T.2–492
Low temperature engineering 621.5
Loyalty Islands   T.2–932
Lumber   674 (670)
Lutes
  music   787 (784 / 787)
Lutheran churches   284 (280 / 284)
Luxembourg   T.2–493
Lymphatic system
  diseases and injuries 616.4 (610)
  physiology   612

M

Macao   T.2–51
Macedonian empire   938 (930 / 938)
Machine engineering 621.8
Machine safety   363.18 (363.1)
Machinery
  engineering   621.8
Macroeconomics   339 (330)
Madagascar   T.2–691
Madeira (Portugal)   T.2–469
Madhya Pradesh (India) T.2–543
Magazines   050
  specific subjects   T.1–05
Magherafelt (N.
  Ireland)   T.2–4162
Magic
  folk literature   398.22 (398.2)
  games   793.8
                 (793 / 793.8)
  occultism   133.4 (130)
Magnetism
  engineering   621.3
  physics   538
Maharashtra (India) T.2–547
Mah-jongg   795.1
                 (793/795.1)
Maine (U.S.A.)   T.2–74
Make-up (Cosmetics) 646.71 (646.7)
Malagasy Republic   T.2–691
Malawi   T.2–6897
Malay languages   499.2
                 (400 / 499.2)
Malaysia   T.2–595
Maldives   T.2–5495
Mali   T.2–66
Malnutrition
  dietetics   613.2 (613)
  social welfare   363.8
Mammals   599 (591 / 599)
  paleozoology   569 (560)
Man, Isle of (England) T.2–427

Man, Prehistoric 573.3 (573)
Management 650
  specific subjects T.1–06
  See also Industry, Labour
    management, Public
    administration
Manchester (England) T.2–427
Manipur (India) T.2–541
Manitoba (Canada) T.2–712
Mankind
  See Human beings
Manners 395
Mansions
  architecture 728.8 (720)
Manufactures 600
Manuscripts 090 (010)
  bibliography 011
Manx language 491.64
    (400 / 491.64)

Maps
  geography 912
  production 526.8
  reading 912.01
  specific subjects T.1–06
Marathi language 491.46
    (400 / 491.46)
Marching band 784.8
    (784 / 784.8)
Marine biology 574.92 (574)
Marine birds 598.3
    (591 / 598.3)
Marine engineering 627
Marine environments T.2–162
Marine resources
  economics 333.9 (333)
Mariology 232 (230)
Maritime Provinces
  (Canada) T.2–715
Marketing 658.8
Marriage
  customs 392 (390)
  law 346 (340)
  sociology 306.8 (306)
Marsupials 599.1
    (591 / 599.1)
Martinique T.2–7298
Mary, Virgin 232 (230)
Maryland (U.S.A.) T.2–75
Mass media
  sociology 302.2 (302)
Mass transit 388.4
Massachusetts (U.S.A.) T.2–74
Materia medica 615.1 (610)
Materials (Engineering) 620.1
Mathematical games 793.7
    (793 / 793.7)
Mathematical geography 526 (520)
Mathematical logic 511.3

Mathematical models
  mathematics 511 (510)
Mathematical physics 530.1 (530)
Mathematics 510
Matrimony
  See Marriage
Matter, States of 530
Marine biology 574.1
Maturation
  animals 591.3 (591)
  humans 612.6 (612)
  plants 581.3 (580)
Mauritania T.2–66
Mauritius T.2–6982
Mayans 972.81 (970)
Mazdaism 295 (290 / 295)
Meals
  cooking 641.5
  planning and service 642 (641)
Meat industry
  agriculture 636
  economics 338.1 (338)
  technology 664 (660)
Mechanical drawing 604.2 (604)
Mechanical engineering 621
Mechanical vibrations 620.3 (620)
Mechanics, Fluid 532
Mechanics (Physics) 531
Mechanics of gases 533 (530)
Mediaeval architecture 723 (720)
Mediaeval history 909.07 (900)
  Europe 940.1 (940)
Mediaeval painting 759.02 (750)
Mediaeval philosophy 189 (100)
Mediaeval sculpture 734 (730)
Medical sciences 610
Medical services
  social welfare 362.1 (362)
Medicine 616 (610)
Mediterranean
  region T.2–1822
Mediterranean Sea T.2–1638
Meghalaya (India) T.2–541
Melanesia T.2–932
Melodrama 792.2 (792)
Menageries 791.8 (791)
Men's voices 782.8 (782)
Mental health 613
Mental illness
  medical aspects 616.89 (610)
  social welfare 362.2 (362)
Mental retardation
  medical aspects 616.89 (610)
  social welfare 362.3 (362)
Mentally handicapped
  persons
  medical aspects 616.89 (610)
  social welfare 362.3 (362)

Merchant marine	387.5 (387)	Minks	
Merseyside (County)	427	animal husbandry	636.9
England	T.2–427		(636/636.9)
Mesopotamia	T.2–35	zoology	599.74
history	935		(591/599.74)
Metabolism	574.1 (574)	Minnesota (U.S.A.)	T.2–77
Metallurgy	669	Minorities	
Metals	669	social welfare	362.8 (362)
engraving	765 (760)	sociology	305.7 (305)
handicrafts	745.56	Miracles	
	(745/745.56)	Christianity	231 (230)
manufacture	671 (670)	other religions	290
metallurgy	669	Mixed voices	782.5 (782)
sculpture	739 (730)	Missions (Religion)	
Metaphysics	110 (100)	Christian	266 (230)
Meteoroids	523.5 (520)	Mississippi (U.S.A.)	T.2–76
Meteorology	551.5	Missouri (U.S.A.)	T.2–77
Methodist churches	287 (280/287)	Mizoram (India)	T.2–541
Mexico	T.2–72	Model-making	
Mezzotinting	766 (760)	handicrafts	745.592
Michigan (U.S.A.)	T.2–77		(745/745.592)
Microbiology	576 (570)	Modern architecture	724 (720)
Microcomputers	004.16 (004)	Modern Greek language	489 (400/489)
Microphotography	778 (770)	Mohammedanism	297 (290/297)
Microscopes		Molecular biology	574.8 (574)
manufacture	681 (680)	animals	591.8 (591)
scientific use	578 (570)	plants	581.8 (580)
Middle Ages	940.1 (940)	Molecular physics	539.6 (539)
Middle East	T.2–56	Moles	599.3
Migrants			(591/599.3)
political science	325 (320)	Mollusks	
sociology	305.9 (305)	animal husbandry	639.4 (639)
Migration (Human)		zoology	594 (591/594)
political science	325 (320)	Monaco	T.2–44
social welfare	362.8 (362)	Monaghan (Republic	
sociology	304.8 (304)	of Ireland)	T.2–4169
Military art and		Monarchy	321 (320)
science	355	Monasticism	255 (230)
Military customs	355.1 (355)	Money	
Military engineering	623	economics	332.4 (332)
Military life	355.1 (355)	numismatics	737 (730)
Military operations		paper printing	769.55 (760)
engineering	623.6 (623)	Monkeys	599.8
military science	355.4 (355)		(591/599.8)
Military science	355	Monks	255 (230)
Military training	355.5 (355)	Monocotyledons	584 (581/584)
Military uniforms	355.1 (355)	Monotremata	599.1
Milk production			(591/599.1)
animal husbandry	637	Montana (U.S.A.)	T.2–78
Mind	153 (150)	Monte Carlo	
Mineralogy	549 (540)	(Monaco)	T.2–44
Minerals		Montserrat	T.2–7297
chemistry	549 (540)	Moon	523.3 (520)
Miniatures		Moral philosophy	170
art	745.592	Moral theology	
	(745/745.592)	Christianity	241 (230)
Miniatures (Painting)	751.7 (750)	other religions	290
Mining engineering	622	Moravian church	284 (280/284)

161

Mormonism	289.3	Museum organization	069 (060)
	(280/289.3)	Museums, Art	708 (700)
Morocco	T.2–642	Music	780
Morphology (Linguistics)	412 (400)	Music appreciation	781.1 (781)
specific languages	T.4–2	Music awards	780.7 (780)
Morphology (Physical		Music competitions	780.7 (780)
structure)	574.1 (574)	Music festivals	780.7 (780)
animals	591.1 (591)	Music halls	792.7 (792)
humans	612.3 (610)	Musical drama	782.1 (782)
plants	581.1 (580)	Musical instruments	782–788 (780)
Mortgaging	332.4 (332)	manufacture	681 (680)
Mosaics	738 (730)	Muslims	297 (290/297)
Moslems		Mysticism	
sociology	305.7 (305)	Christianity	248 (230)
theology	297 (290)	religion	200
Mosses	588 (581/588)	Mythology	398
Motion pictures		religious	200
entertainment	791.43 (791)		
photography	778.5 (770)	**N**	
Motor sports	796.7	Nagaland (India)	T.2–541
	(796/796.7)	Nagar Haveli (India)	T.2–547
Motorboats		Nails (Human anatomy)	
technology	623.8	diseases and injury	616.5 (610)
Motorcars	629.2	physiology	612
sports	796.7	Names, Personal	929.4 (929)
	(796/796.7)	Namibia	T.2–688
transportation	388.3 (388)	Napoleonic period	
Motorcycles	629.2	European history	940.27 (940)
sports	796.7	French history	944.05 (944)
	(796/796.7)	Narcotic habit	
transportation	388.3 (388)	ethics	178 (170)
Motortrucks	629.2	health	613.8 (613)
transportation	388.3 (388)	Natal (South Africa)	T.2–684
Mountaineering	796.52	National income	339 (330)
	(796/796.52)	National parks	333.7 (333)
Mountains (Physiographic		National states	321 (320)
feature)	T.2–143	Nationalism	320
Mourne (N. Ireland)	T.2–4165	Natural disasters	
Moving pictures		history	904 (900)
entertainment	791.4 (791)	social welfare	363.3
photography	778.5 (770)	Natural history	508 (500)
Moyle (N. Ireland)	T.2–4161	Natural religion	210 (200)
Mozambique	T.2–679	Natural resources	
Muhammedanism	297 (290/297)	conservation	639.9 (639)
Mules (Animals)		economics	333.7 (333)
animal husbandry	636.1 (636)	geology	553 (551)
zoology	599.725	Nature trails	574.07
	(591/599.725)	birds	598.07
Municipal engineering	628	botany	580.7
Municipalities		zoology	590.7
public administration	352 (350)	Naturopathy	615.5 (610)
Munster (Republic of		Nautical almanacs	520
Ireland)	T.2–419	Nautical engineering	623.8
Murals	751.7 (750)	Naval engineering	623.8
Murder	364	Naval warfare	359 (355)
Muscles		Navies	359 (355)
diseases and injuries	616.7 (610)	Navigation	623.8
physiology	612.7 (612)	Navigation, Celestial	527

Near East	T.2–56	Non-verbal communication	419
Nebraska (U.S.A.)	T.2–78	Norfolk (England)	T.2–426
Nebulas	523.1 (520)	North Africa	T.2–6
Necromancy	133.4 (130)	North America	T.2–7
Needlepoint	746.44 (746)	North American native	
Needlework		languages	497 (400 / 497)
home economics	646.2	North Carolina (U.S.A.)	T.2–75
textile arts	746.4 (746)	North Dakota (U.S.A.)	T.2–78
Needy people		North Down (N. Ireland)	T.2–4165
social welfare	362.5 (362)	North Pole	T.2–1632
Negro Africa	T.2–67	North Scotland	T.2–4111
Neighbourhoods	307	North Yorkshire	
Neoplasms	616.9 (610)	(England)	T.2–428
Nepal	T.2–5496	Northamptonshire	
Nervous system		(England)	T.2–425
diseases and injuries	616.8 (610)	Northern hemisphere	T.2–1813
physiology	612.8 (612)	Northern Ireland (U.K.)	
Netball	796.32	area number	T.2–416
	(796 / 796.32)	history	941.6
Netherlandish languages	439.3 (400)	See also British Isles,	
Netherlands	T.2–492	United Kingdom	
Nevada (U.S.A.)	T.2–79	Northern Rhodesia	T.2–6894
New Brunswick		Northern Territories	
(Canada)	T.2–715	(Canada)	T.2–719
New Caledonia	T.2–932	Northumberland	
New Guinea	T.2–95	(England)	T.2–428
New Hampshire		Norway	T.2–481
(U.S.A.)	T.2–74	Norwegian language	439.9
New Hebrides	T.2–932		(400 / 439.9)
New Jersey (U.S.A.)	T.2–74	Nose	612.86 (612)
New Mexico (U.S.A.)	T.2–78	Notations	
New South Wales	T.2–944	linguistics	411 (400)
New Testament	225	specific languages	T.4–11
New York (U.S.A.)	T.2–747	music	781.4 (781)
New Zealand	T.2–931	Nottinghamshire	
Newfoundland		(England)	T.2–425
(Canada)	T.2–718	Nova Scotia	
Newry and Mourne		(Canada)	T.2–716
(N. Ireland)	T.2–4165	Novels	800
Newspapers	070	collections	808.83 (800)
for collections See serials		compositions	808.3 (800)
Newtonabbey		criticism	808.3 (800)
(N. Ireland)	T.2–4161	specific literatures	T.3–3
Nicaragua	T.2–7285	Nuclear engineering	621.48
Nicobar Islands (India)	T.2–548	Nuclear physics	539.7 (539)
Niger	T.2–66	Nuclear reactions	539.7 (539)
Nigeria	T.2–669	Nuclear warfare	355.4 (355)
Nightclub performances	792.7 (792)	Number games	793.7
Nobility			(793 / 793.7)
genealogy	929.7 (929)	Number theory	512
sociology	305.3 (305)	Numerology	133.3 (130)
Noise		Numismatics	737 (730)
social problem	363.74 (363.7)	Nuns	255 (230)
Noise control	620.2 (620)	Nursery rhymes	
Non-combat services	355.3 (355)	folk literature	398.5
Non-ferrous metals		Nursing	
manufacture	673 (670)	home economics	649.8 (649)
metallurgy	669	medicine	610.73 (610)

Nutrition
  home economics 641
  personal hygiene 613.2 (613)
  physiology 612.3 (612)
Nyasaland T.2–6897

O

Objets trouvés 745.58
  (745 / 745.58)
Oboes
  music 788 (784 / 788)
Obscenity
  ethics 176 (170)
  public morals 363.4
Observatories
  astronomy 522 (520)
Obstetrics 618.1 (610)
Occultism 133 (130)
Occupational diseases 616.9 (610)
Occupational ethics 174 (170)
Occupational hazards 363.11 (363.1)
Occupational safety 363.11 (363.1)
Occupations 331
Ocean transportation 387.3 (387)
Oceanography 551.4 (551)
Oceans (Physiographic
  feature) T.2–162
  See also specific oceans
Office equipment 651.2 (651)
Office management 651
Office services 651
Ohio (U.S.A.) T.2–77
Oils
  chemical technology 665 (660)
  painting 751 (750)
Oklahoma (U.S.A.) T.2–76
Old English language 429
Old age
  social welfare 362.6 (362)
Old Testament 221
Oligarchies 321 (320)
Olympic games (Summer) 796.48
  (796 / 796.48)
Olympic games (Winter) 796.98
  (796 / 796.98)
Omagh (N. Ireland) T.2–4162
Oman T.2–53
Ontario (Canada) T.2–713
Ontology 111 (100)
Opera 782.1 (782)
Operettas 782.1 (782)
Ophthalmology 617.7 (610)
Optics
  physics 535
Orange Free State
  (South Africa) T.2–685
Oratorios 782.2 (782)
Oratory 808.51 (808)

Orchards 634
Orchestras 784.2
  (784 / 784.2)
Orchids 584 (580 / 584)
Orders and decorations 929.9 (929)
Ordnance
  military science 355.4 (355)
  technology 623.4 (623)
Oregon (U.S.A.) T.2–79
Organic chemistry 547 (540)
Organic evolution 575 (570)
Organs (Anatomy) See
  Anatomy
Organs (Musical instrument)
  music 786.5
  (784 / 786.5)
Organizations and clubs 366
  specific subjects T.1–06
Oriental architecture 722 (720)
Oriental churches
  Christianity 281 (280 / 281)
Oriental philosophy 181 (100)
Oriental sculpture 732 (730)
Orienteering 796.5
  (796 / 796.5)
Original sin 233 (230)
Orissa (India) T.2–541
Oriya language 491.46
  (400 / 491.46)
Ornamental plants 635.9
Ornithology 598 (591 / 598)
Orphans
  social welfare 362.7 (362)
Orthodox churches
  (Christian) 281.9
  (280 / 281.9)
Osteopathy 610
  therapeutic system 615.5 (610)
Ostriches 598.5
  (591 / 598.5)
Otology 617.8 (610)
Otters 599.74
  (591 / 599.74)
Outdoor games 796
Outdoor life 796.5
  (796 / 796.5)
Outer space T.2–19
Over-population 363.9 (363)
Owls 598.9
  (591 / 598.9)
Oxfordshire (England) T.2–425
Oysters
  animal husbandry 639.4 (639)
  zoology 594 (591 / 594)

P

Pacific Ocean T.2–164
Pacific Ocean region T.2–1823

Pacifism
ethics 172 (170)
political science 320
sociology 303.6 (303)
Packaging technology 688.8 (680)
Paediatrics 681.92 (610)
Paenungulata 599.6
(591/599.6)
Pageants 791.6 (791)
Painting (Art) 750
textiles 746.6 (746)
Pakistan T.2–5491
Palaces
architecture 728.8 (720)
Paleobotany 561 (560)
Paleontology 560
Paleosiberian languages 494 (400/494)
Paleozoology 562 (560)
Palestine
ancient area number T.2–33
modern area number T.2–5694
history to 70 A.D. 933 (930/933)
history from 70 A.D. 956.94 (950)
Palmistry 133.3 (130)
Palms (Plant) 584 (580/584)
Pampas T.2–153
Panama T.2–7287
Panjab (India) T.2–545
Panjabi language 491.42
(400/491.42)
Pantomime 792.3 (792)
Papacy 282 (280/282)
Paper
handicrafts 745.54
(745/745.54)
manufacture 676 (670)
Paper money
currency 332.4 (332)
prints 769.55 (760)
Papua New Guinea T.2–95
Parachuting (Sport) 797.5
(796/797.5)
Parades 791.6 (791)
Paraguay T.2–892
Paranormal phenomena 130
Paraphotic phenomena
engineering 621.36 (621.3)
physics 535
Parapsychology 133 (130)
Parent and child
social relations 306.8 (306)
Parenting 649.1 (649)
Parish organization 250 (230)
Parks 711
Parliaments 328 (320)
Parrots
zoology 598.7
(591/598.7)

Parseeism 295 (290/295)
Parsi language 491.5
(400/491.5)
Partially-sighted persons
medical aspects 617.7 (610)
social welfare 362.41 (362)
Party games 793.2
(793/793.2)
Passeriformes 598.8
(591/598.8)
Pastoral care
education 371.4
Pastoral theology
Christianity 253 (230)
Patchwork 746.46
(746/746.46)
Patents 608
Pathology 574.1
animals
veterinary science 636.089
zoology 591.1 (591)
humans 616 (610)
plants 581.1 (580)
Pawnbroking 332.7 (332)
Peace movements 303.6 (303)
Peace studies
sociology 303.6 (303)
Pediatrics 618.92 (610)
Penmanship 411 (400)
Pennsylvania (U.S.A.) T.2–74
Penology 364
Pentecostal Assemblies 289.9
(280/289.9)
Perching birds 598.8
(591/598.8)
Percussion instruments
music 786.8
(784/786.8)
Performing arts 790.2 (790)
Perfumes
technology 668 (660)
Periodicals 050
specific subjects T.1–05
Persia See Iran
Persian languages 491.5
(400/491.5)
Personal appearance
customs 391 (390)
home economics 646.71 (646.7)
Personal grooming 646.71 (646.7)
Personal hygiene 613
Personal living 646.7
Personal names 929.4 (929)
Perspective 742 (740)
Personnel management 658.3 (658)
Peru T.2–85
Pesticides
chemical technology 668 (660)

165

Pest control	363.78 (363.7)	Pirates	910
Pests		Pisces *See* Fishes	
agriculture	632 (630)	Plains	T.2–145
economic biology	574.6 (574)	Plane regions	
economic botany	581.6 (580)	(Physiographic	
economic zoology	591.6 (591)	feature)	T.2–145
social aspects	363.78 (363.7)	Planets	523.4 (520)
Petroleum		Planned economics	330.1 (330)
economic geology	553 (551)	Plantagenet dynasty	942.03 (942)
exploration	622	Plant management	658.2 (658)
extraction	622	Plants	
processing	665 (660)	agriculture	630
Petrology	551	botany	580
Pets	636.088 (636)	diseases, injuries, pests	632 (630)
Pharmacology	615.1 (610)	Plants (Factories)	
Philanthropy		management	658.2 (658)
ethics	177 (170)	Plastic arts	730
Philately	769.56 (760)	Plastics	668 (660)
Philippines	T.2–599	handicrafts	745.57
Philology	400		(745/745.57)
Philosophy	100	Plate tectonics	551.2 (551)
specific subjects	T.1–01	Plateaus	T.2–143
Phonetics	414 (400)	Plato	182 (100)
Phonology	414 (400)	Plays (Texts) *See* Drama	
specific languages	T.4–15	Plots (Literature)	800
Phonorecords	T.1–0208	Plumbing	696 (690)
Photography	770	Plutonic phenomena	551.2 (551)
Physical anthropology	573	Pneumatic engineering	621.5
Physical appearance	646.71 (646.7)	Poetry	
Physical chemistry	541 (540)	collections	808.81 (808)
Physical education		composition	808.1 (808)
primary education	372 (370)	criticism	809.1 (809)
secondary education	796.07	specific literatures	T.3–1
Physical exercise		Poisons	615.9 (610)
medical aspects	613.7 (613)	Poland	T.2–438
sports	796	Police services	363.2
Physical fitness	613.7 (613)	Polish language	491.85
Physical geography	910.02 (910)		(400/491.85)
Physically-disabled persons		Political parties	324 (320)
social welfare	362.4 (362)	Political process	324 (320)
Physicians	610.92 (610)	Political science	320
Physics	530	Pollution	
Physiological psychology	152 (150)	social welfare	363.73 (363.7)
Physiology	574.1	Polo	796.353
animals	591.1 (591)		(796/796.353)
humans	612	Polyglot dictionaries	
Piano		linguistics	413 (400)
music	786.2	specific subjects	T.1–03
	(784/786.2)	Polymers	
Pickling (Cooking)	641.6 (641.5)	chemical technology	668 (660)
Pictures	T.1–022	Polynesia	T.2–96
art	700–770	Polynesian languages	499 (400/499)
Pigeons	598.6	Pondicherry	
	(591/598.6)	(India)	T.2–548
Pigs		Pool (Game)	794.7
animal husbandry	636.4 (636)		(793/794.7)
zoology	599.73	Pop art	709.04 (700)
	(591/599.73)	Pop music	781.75 (781)

Popular music	781.74 (781)	Preying birds	598.9
Population			(591/598.9)
movement	304.8 (304)	Price lists	T.1–029
problems	364	Primary education	372 (370)
statistics	310	Primary industries	338.2 (338)
Porcelain		Primates	599.8
art	738 (730)		(591/599.8)
technology	666 (660)	Prince Edward Island	
Pornography		(Canada)	T.2–717
ethics	176 (170)	Printmaking	760
public morals	363.4	Printing	686.2 (680)
Porpoises	599.5	Printing (Textiles)	746.6 (746)
	(591/599.5)	Prints	769.1 (760)
Ports		Prisons	365 (364)
water transportation	387.1 (387)	Private law	346 (340)
Portugal	T.2–469	Probabilities	519
philosophers	196 (100)	Problem children	
Portuguese language	469 (400/469)	education	371.9 (370)
Postage stamps		family life	649.1 (649)
collecting	769.56 (760)	Product hazards	363.19 (363.1)
Postal communication	383	Production economics	338
Potatoes	633	Production management	658.5 (658)
Potholing	796.525	Professional ethics	174 (170)
	(796/796.525)	Programming (Computers)	005 (004)
		Programs (Computers)	005 (004)
Pottery		Pronunciation	414 (400)
ceramic arts	738 (730)	specific languages	T.4–15
technology	666 (660)	Prose	
Poultry	636.5 (636)	collections	808.88 (808)
Poverty	362.5	composition	808.4 (808)
	(362/362.5)	criticism	809.4 (809)
Power supply		specific literatures	T.3–4
social aspects	363.62 (363.6)	Prospecting	622
utilities	697 (690)	Prostitution	
Powys (Wales)	T.2–4292	ethics	176 (170)
Prairie Provinces		social control	363.4
(Canada)	T.2–712	sociology	306.7 (306)
Prairies (Physiographic		Protestant churches	284 (280/284)
feature)	T.2–153	Protozoa	593 (591/593)
Prayer	200	Proverbs	
Christianity	248 (230)	folk literature	398.5
other religions	290	Pseudepigrapha	229.8
Precious metals		Psychiatry	616.89 (610)
art	739.2 (730)	Psychic phenomena	133.8 (130)
Precision instruments	681 (680)	Psychology	150
Pregnancy	618.1 (610)	Puberty See Adolescence	
Prehistoric life	560	Public administration	350
animals	562	Public buildings	
humans	930	architecture	725 (720)
plants	561	Public education	379 (370)
Prehistoric man	573	Public finance	336 (330)
Presbyterian churches	285 (280/285)	Public health	614
Preservation		Public households	
antiques	745.1 (745)	management	647
art	702 (700)	Public law	342 (340)
museology	069 (060)	Public morals	363.4
paintings	751.6 (750)	Public opinion	303
See also Conservation		Public performances	791
Press	070		

Public relations	659	Radioactive waste, Disposal of	
Public safety	363.1	social problem	363.17 (363.1)
Public speaking	808.51 (808)	technology	621.48
Public utilities		Ragtime	781.76 (781)
economics	333.7 (333)	Railroads *See* Railways	
social welfare	363.6	Railways	
Public welfare	360	engineering	625.1
Public worship		safety	363.122 (363.1)
Christianity	264 (230)	transportation	385
Publishing	070	Rajasthan (India)	T.2–544
Puerto Rico	T.2–7295	Rajasthani language	491.47
Pulp			(400 / 491.47)
manufacture	676	Rare birds	598.04
Punjab (India)	T.2–545		(591 / 598.04)
Punjabi language	491.42	Rare books	090 (010)
	(400 / 491.42)	bibliography	011
Puppetry	791.5 (790)	Rare species	
Puzzles	793.7	animals	591.04 (591)
	(793 / 793.7)	birds	598.04 (598)
folk literature	398.5	plants	580
Puritanism	285 (280 / 285)	Rationalism	
		philosophy	100
Q		religion	210 (200)
		Rats	
Qatar	T.2–53	agricultural pests	632 (630)
Quakers	289.6	zoology	599.3
	(280 / 289.6)		(591/599.3)
Quantum theory	530	Reading	028
Quarrying	622	education	372 (370)
Quebec (Canada)	T.2–714	hobby	790.138
Queensland (Australia)	T.2–943		(790.1)
Quilting	746.46 (746)	rhetoric	808.54 (800)
Quotations	080 (010)	Real estate market	
literature	808 (800)	economics	333.1 (333)
specific literatures	T.3–8	Reasoning	153 (150)
Qwaqwa (South Africa)	T.2–6859	Recipes	641.5–56
		Recitation	808.54 (808)
R		Recording (Sound)	
		music	781.4 (781)
Rabbits		Records management	
animal husbandry	636.9 (636)	office practice	651.5 (651)
zoology	599.3	Recreation	790.1
	(591 / 599.3)	safety	363.14 (363.1)
Races (Human)	573	Red Cross	361.7 (361)
Races (Sports)	796	Reformation (Christian)	270 (230)
animals	798 (796/798)	European history	940.23 (940)
Racism	305.7 (305)	*See also* Reformed	
Rackets (Game)	796.343	churches	
	(796 / 796.343)	Reformed churches	284 (280 / 284)
Racoons	599.74	Refrigeration	
	(591/599.74)	engineering	621.5
Radiation		food technology	664 (660)
physics	539.2 (539)	home economics	641.4 (641)
Radio		Refuse	
communication	384.5 (384)	social services	363.72 (363.7)
engineering	621.384	technology	604.6 (604)
	(621.38)	Relativity	530
music	781.5 (781)	Relief (Welfare)	360
performing arts	791.44 (791)		

Relief processes
  graphic arts 761 (760)
Religion 200
  See also entries beginning
    with Religious
Religion and art 704 (700)
  Christianity 246 (230)
  painting 755 (750)
Religion and science 215 (200)
Religion and society
  Christian social
    theology 261 (230)
  sociology 306.4 (306)
Religion and state 261 (230)
Religious buildings
  architecture 726 (720)
Religious congregations
  See specific religions
Religious music
  music 781.6 (781)
  religious services 264 (230)
Religious orders
  (Christianity) 255 (230)
Religious subjects (Art) 704 (700)
  Christian 246 (230)
  painting 755 (750)
Religious training
  Christianity 268 (230)
Reminiscences 920
  specific subjects T.1–092
Remote control engineering 629.8
Renaissance
  architecture 724.1 (720)
  art 709.024 (700)
  European history 940.21 (940)
  painting 759.03 (750)
Renting 333.1 (333)
Reproduction (Organisms) 574.1 (574)
  animals 591.3 (591)
  humans 613.3 (613)
    diseases 616.6 (610)
    physiology 612.6 (612)
  plants 581.1 (580)
Reprography 652 (651)
Reptiles
  animal husbandry 639.3 (639)
  paleozoology 567 (560)
  zoology 597.9
    (591/597.9)
Republic of South
  Africa T.2–68
Republics 321 (320)
Rescue work
  naval technology 623.8
  social services 363.1
Research 001.4 (001)
Resins
  chemical technology 668 (660)

Respiratory system
  diseases and injuries 616.2 (610)
  physiology 612.2 (612)
Rest 613.7 (613)
Restaurants 647
Restoration 069 (060)
  buildings 690.28 (690)
  paintings 751.6 (750)
Retailing 658.8
Retreats (Religion)
  Christian 269 (230)
Revelation
  Bible 228 (225)
Revivals (Religion) 269 (230)
Revolution
  sociology 303.6 (303)
  See also specific countries
Rhetoric 808
Rhinoceroses 599.72
    (591/599.72)
Rhode Island (U.S.A.) T.2–74
Rhodesia T.2–689
Rice
  crop 633
  plant 584 (580/584)
Riddles
  entertainment 793.7 (793)
  folk literature 398.5
Rifles
  technology 623.4 (623)
Rites and ceremonies
  Christianity 264 (230)
River Thames T.2–422
Rivers T.2–169
  transportation 386.3 (386)
Roads
  engineering 625.7
  safety 363.125
  transportation 388.1 (388)
Robots 629.8
Rock climbing 796.52
    (796/796.52)
Rock 'n' roll 781.65
    (781.64)
Rockets
  military science 355.4 (355)
  technology 623.4 (623)
Rocks 551
Rococo painting 759.04 (750)
Rodents
  agricultural pests 632 (630)
  zooogy 599.3
    (591/599.3)
Roller skating 796.1
    (796/796.1)
Rolling stock 625.1
Roman Britain 936.1
    (930/936.1)

Roman Catholic church	282 (280 / 282)
Roman empire	937 (930 / 937)
Roman philosophy	187 (100)
Roman sculpture	733 (730)
Roman walls (Great Britain)	936.1 (930 / 936.1)
Romance languages	440 (400 / 440)
Romanesque painting	759.02 (750)
Rome	
ancient area number	T.2–37
modern area number	T.2–45
history to 476 A.D.	937
history from 476 A.D.	945
Romany language	491.49 (400 / 491.49)
Roses	583 (580 / 583)
Roulette	795.1 (793 / 795.1)
Royalty	
genealogy	927.7 (929)
sociology	305.5 (305)
Rubber	
handicrafts	745 (745 / 745.47)
manufacture	678 (670)
technology	668 (660)
Rubbish collection	363.72 (363.7)
Rugby football	796.333 (796 / 796.333)
Rugs and carpets	
arts	746.7 (746)
home economics	643.3 (643)
textile production	677 (670)
Ruminants	636.2 (636)
Rural areas	T.2–1734
sociology	307.72 (307)
Russia	
area number	T.2–47
history	947
philosophers	197 (100)
Russian language	491.7 (400 / 491.7)
Russian literature	891.7
Russian Orthodox Church	281.9 (280 / 281.9)
Russian Revolution (1917)	947.084 (947)
Rwanda	T.2–67

S

Sacraments (Christian)	265 (230)
Sacred books	
Christianity	220
Islam	297.8 (290 / 297.8)
Judaism	221
Sacred buildings	
architecture	726 (720)
Sacred music	
music	781.6 (781)
religious services	264 (230)
vocal	782.2 (782)
Safety	363.1
See also specific subjects	
Safety law	344 (340)
Safety, Personal	613.6 (613)
Sagas	398.22 (398.2)
Saguia el Hamna	T.2–648
Sahara	T.2–648
Sahara Desert	T.2–66
Sailboating	797.1 (796 / 797.1)
Sailing	
navigation	623.8
sports	797.1 (796 / 797.1)
Saint Christopher Island	T.2–7297
Saint Helena Island	T.2–973
Saint Kitts Island	T.2–7297
Saint Lucia Island	T.2–7298
Saint Vincent Island	T.2–7298
Saints	
Christianity	235 (230)
Saints' days	
Christianity	263 (230)
Salamanders	597.6 (591 / 597.6)
Salesmanship	658.8
Salvation and grace	
Christianity	234 (230)
Salvation Army	287 (280 / 287)
Samoa	T.2–96
Sampling (Mathematics)	519.5 (519)
Sandpipers	598.3 (591 / 598.3)
Sanitary engineering	628
Sanitation	363.72 (363.7)
home economics	644 (643)
technology	628
Saskatchewan (Canada)	T.2–712
Satellites (Astronomy)	532.2 (520)
Satellites, Artificial	629.4
Satire	800
specific literatures	T.3–7
Saudi Arabia	T.2–53
Savings and investment	332.6 (332)
Savings banks	332.1 (332)
Saxophones (Music)	788 (784 / 788)
Scandinavia	T.2–48
Scholarship	001
Schools See Education	
Schizophyta	589.9 (580 / 589.9)
Science	500
Science and religion	215 (200)

Scientific recreations 793.8
    (793 / 793.8)
Scientists 509.2 (500)
Scilly Isles (British
    Isles) T.2–423
Scotland
  ancient area number T.2–361
  modern area number T.2–411
  history to 5th century A.D. 936.1
  history from 5th
    century A.D. 941.1
  See also British Isles,
    United Kingdom
Scottish Gaelic 491.63
    (400 / 491.63)
Scottish Highlands T.2–4111
Screen process printing 764 (760)
Sculpture 730
Sea birds 598.3
    (591 / 598.3)
Sea warfare and forces 359 (355)
Seals (Animals) 599.74
    (591 / 599.74)
Seals (Devices)
  genealogy 929.8 (929)
  numismatics 737 (730)
Seamanship 623.8
Seaport facilities
  commerce 387.1
  technology 627
Seas (Oceanography) 551.4 (551)
Seas (Physiographic
  feature) T.2–162
Seasons
  astronomy 525 (520)
Secondary education 373
Secondary industries 338.4 (338)
Secret service 351 (350)
Secret societies 366
Secretarial services 651.3 (651)
Secretive organs
  diseases 616.4 (610)
  physiology 612.4 (612)
Sects (Religion)
  Christianity 280
  other religions 290
Secular clergy 253 (230)
Secular songs 782.4 (782)
Security exchanges 332.6 (332)
Seed-bearing plants 582 (580 / 582)
Seedless plants 586 (580 / 586)
Segregation
  political science 321 (320)
  sociology 305
Seismology 551.2 (551)
Self 155 (150)
Self-education 374 (370)
Self-respect 155 (150)

Semantics 412
  specific languages T.4–2
Semiconductivity 537.6 (537)
Semitic languages 492 (400 / 492)
Senegal T.2–66
Sense organs
  diseases and injuries 616.8 (610)
  physiology 612
Serials 050
  specific subjects T.1–05
Serigraphy 764 (760)
Sermons
  Christian 250 (230)
Serpents 597.9
    (591 / 597.9)
Servomechanisms 629.8
Set theory 511.3
Seventh Day
  Adventists 286 (280 / 286)
Sewage treatment 628
Sewing (Needlework)
  home economics 646.2
  textile arts 746.4 (746)
Sex
  behaviour
    ethics 176 (170)
    social aspects 306.7 (306)
  differentiation
    education 376 (370)
  discrimination 305.3 (305)
  grouping 305.3 (305)
  organs 612
  pyschology 155 (150)
Sexism 305.3 (305)
Sexual techniques 613.9 (613)
Seychelles T.2–696
Sharks 597.3
    (591 / 597.3)
Sheep
  animal husbandry 636.3 (636)
  zoology 599.73
    (591 / 599.73)
Shells (Art) 745.55
    (745 / 745.55)
Shetland Islands
  (Scotland) T.2–4111
Shintoism 299 (290 / 299)
Shipping
  transportation 387.5 (387)
Ships
  naval technology 623.8
  transportation 387.2 (387)
Shoes
  manufacture 685 (680)
Shooting
  sport 799.2–3
    (796 / 799.2–.3)
Shops, Retail 658.8

171

Short stories		
collections	808.83 (800)	
composition	808.3 (800)	
criticism	809.3 (800)	
specific literatures	T.3–3	
Shorthand	653 (651)	
Shrines		
Christianity	240 (230)	
other religions	290	
Shropshire (England)	T.2–424	
Shrubs		
botany	582 (580 / 582)	
floriculture	635.9	
Siberia	T.2–57	
Sick people		
social welfare	362.1 (362)	
Sierra Leone	T.2–664	
Sight		
diseases and injuries	617.7 (610)	
physiology	612	
Sign language	419 (400)	
Signals	001	
Signs and symbols	001	
Sikhism	294.6	
	(290 / 294.6)	
Sikkim	T.2–541	
Silk screen printing	764 (760)	
Silkworms	638	
Silos	631.2 (630)	
Silversmithing	739.2 (730)	
Simple machines		
technology	600	
Sin		
Christianity	230	
other religions	290	
Sinai Peninsula	T.2–53	
Singapore	T.2–595	
Singing	782	
Singing games	796.1	
	(796 / 796.1)	
Single people		
sociology	305.9 (305)	
Single-sex education	376 (370)	
Sinhalese language	491.48	
	(400 / 491.48)	
Sinitic languages	495 (400 / 495)	
Sino-Tibetan languages	495 (400 / 495)	
Sirenia	599.5	
	(591 / 599.5)	
Skating, Ice	796.9	
	(796 / 796.9)	
Skating, Roller	796.1	
	(796 / 796.1)	
Skeletal system	611 (612)	
diseases and injuries	616.7 (610)	
Sketching	741 (740)	
Skiing (Snow)	796.9	
	(796 / 796.9)	
Skiing (Water)	797.3	
	(796 / 797.3)	
Skill, Games of	794 (793 / 794)	
Skilled workers	331.1 (331)	
Skin		
diseases and injuries	616.5 (610)	
physiology	612.7 (612)	
Skindiving		
sports	793.3	
	(796 / 797.3)	
Slang	417 (400)	
specific languages	T.4–7	
Slavery		
ethics	177 (170)	
political science	326 (320)	
Slavic languages	491.8	
	(400 / 491.8)	
Sleep		
hygiene	613.7 (613)	
psychology	154 (150)	
Slimming	613.2 (613)	
Slovakia	T.2–437	
Slow learners	371.9 (370)	
Slugs (Animals)	594 (591/594)	
Slums	307	
Small-group behaviour	302.3 (302)	
Smell	612.86 (612)	
Smokers' supplies		
manufacture	688 (680)	
Smoking		
addiction	613.8 (613)	
Snails	594 (591 / 594)	
Snakes	597.9	
	(591 / 597.9)	
Snooker	794.7	
	(793 / 794.7)	
Snow and ice sports	796.9	
	(796 / 796.9)	
Snowmobiling	796.9	
	(796 / 796.9)	
Soap		
technology	668 (660)	
Soccer	796.334	
	(796 / 796.334)	
Social adjustment	302.5 (302)	
Social anthropology	306	
Social aggregates	305	
Social behaviour		
personal living	646.71 (646.7)	
Social change	303.4 (303)	
Social interaction	302	
Social classes	305.5 (305)	
Social conflict	303.6 (303)	
Social control	303	
Social forecasts	303.4	
Social groups	305	
Social institutions	306	
Social law	344 (340)	

172

Social mobility 305
Social problems and services 360
Social psychology 302
Social relations
  ethics 177 (170)
  sociology 302
Social sciences 300
Social security 368 (360)
Social services 362–363
Social stratification 305
Social structure 305
Social studies 300
Social theology 261 (230)
Social welfare 361
Social work 361.3 (361)
Socialism
  economics 330
  political science 320
Socialization 303
Socially handicapped
  children 362.8 (362)
Society of Friends 289.6
    (280/289.6)
Socioeconomic classes 305.5 (305)
Sociobiology 304.5 (304)
Sociolinguistics 302.2 (302)
Sociology 301
Sociology of war 303.6 (303)
Sociology, Rural 307.72 (307)
Sociology, Urban 307.76 (307)
Socratic philosophy 182 (100)
Software (Computers) 005 (004)
Soil
  conservation 631.4 (630)
  erosion 551.3 (551)
  science 631.4 (630)
Solar energy
  technology 621.4
Solar system 523.2 (520)
Solar wind 523.5 (520)
Soldiers 356 (355)
Solids, Mechanics of 531
Solomon Islands T.2–932
Somalia T.2–67
Somerset (England) T.2–423
Sonatas 781.8 (781)
Songs 782.42 (782)
Sorcery 133.4 (130)
Soteriology
  Christian 234 (230)
Sound
  building 690
  engineering 620.2 (620)
  physics 534
South Africa T.2–68
South America T.2–8
South American native
  languages 498 (400/498)

South Australia T.2–942
South Carolina (U.S.A.) T.2–75
South Dakota (U.S.A.) T.2–78
South Indian Ocean
  islands T.2–69
South Island (New
  Zealand) T.2–9315
South Ndebele (South
  Africa) T.2–6829
South Pole T.2–989
South Wales (Great
  Britain) T.2–4292
South Yorkshire (County)
  England T.2–428
Southeast Asia T.2–59
Southern hemisphere T.2–1814
Southern Rhodesia T.2–6891
Soviet Union T.2–47
Space (Extra-terrestrial) T.2–19
  flight 629.4
  stations 629.4
  transportation 387.8 (387.7)
Spain
  ancient area number T.2–366
  modern area number T.2–46
  history to 415 A.D. 936.6 (930)
  history from 415 A.D. 946
  painters 759.6
  philosophers 196 (100)
Spanish language 460 (400/460)
Spanish literature 860
Sparrows 598.8
    (591/598.8)
Special education 371.9 (370)
Spectroscopy 535.8 (535)
Speech disorders 618.8 (610)
Speeches
  collections 808.85 (808)
  composition 808.5 (808)
  criticism 809.5 (809)
  specific literatures T.3–5
Spelling 411 (40)
  specific languages T.4–15
Spermatophyta 582 (580/582)
Spherical astronomy 522 (520)
Spiders 595 (591/595)
Spinal cord 612.82 (612)
Spiritual beings
  Christianity 235 (230)
Spiritual life 200
  Christianity 240 (230)
Spiritual renewal
  Christianity 269 (230)
Spiritualism 133.9 (130)
Sponges 593 (591/593)
Sports 796
  ethics 175 (170)
  hazards 363.14 (363.1)

173

Sportsmanship	175 (170)	Style, Literary	800
Squash (Game)	793.343	Subconscious	154 (150)
	(796 / 796.343)	Subcultures	306.1 (306)
Squirrels	599.3	Subject bibliographies	016 (011)
	(591/599.3)	Submarine geology	551.4 (551)
Sri Lanka	T.2–5493	Submarines	
Staff associations		military science	359 (355)
labour economics	331.88 (331)	technology	623.8
Staffordshire (England)	T.2–424	Subsonics	620.2 (620)
Stamps (Postage)		Subsurface resources	
graphic arts	769.56 (760)	economics	333.79 (333)
philately	769.56 (760)	Suburban communities	306.76 (306)
Stars		Subways	388.4
astronomy	523.8 (520)	Success	646.7
State (Political entity)	321 (320)	Succession (Law)	346 (340)
Statistical mathematics	519.5 (519)	Sudan	T.2–624
Statistics	310	Suffolk (England)	T.2–426
specific subjects	T.1–02	Suffrage	324 (320)
Stealing	364	Suicide	364
Steam engineering	621.1	Sun	523.7 (520)
Steel		Sunday	263 (230)
metallurgy	669	Sunday schools	268 (230)
technology	672 (670)	Superconductivity	537.6 (537)
Stepmothers		Supermarkets	658.8
sociology	306.8 (306)	Supernatural, The	
Steppes	T.2–145	folk literature	398.25 (398.2)
Stewart Island (New		occultism	130
Zealand)	T.2–9315	Superstitions	
Stock exchanges	332.6 (332)	folklore	398
Stock breeding	636.08 (636)	Surface processes (Geology)	551.3 (551)
Stock market	332.6 (332)	Surfing	797.3
Stomach			(796 / 797.3)
diseases and injuries	616.3 (610)	Surgery	617 (610)
physiology	612	Surinam	T.2–883
Stone age	930.1 (930)	Surrey (England)	T.2–422
Stones	551	Surveying	526.9 (520)
Storage of food		Suspense plays	792.2 (792)
home economics	641.4 (641)	Sussex (England)	T.2–422
technology	664 (660)	Swahili language	496 (400 / 496)
Storms	551.6	Swaziland	T.2–6813
Storytelling	808.54 (808)	Sweden	T.2–485
Strabane (N. Ireland)	T.2–4162	Swedish language	439.7
Strategy and tactics (Military)	355		(400 / 439.7)
Strathclyde (Scotland)	T.2–414	Swimming	797.2
Stratification (Geological)	551.7 (551)		(796 / 797.2)
Stratification (Social)	305.5 (305)	Swine	
Stratigraphy	551.7 (551)	animal husbandry	636.4 (636)
Strigiformes	598.9	zoology	599.73
	(591 / 598.9)		(591 / 599.73)
Strikes	331.8 (331)	Switzerland	T.2–494
Stringed instruments (Music)	787 (784 / 787)	Symbolic logic	511.3
Structural engineering	624.1 (624)	Symbolism	001
Structural geology	551.8 (551)	Symphony orchestras	784.2
Stuarts	941.06 (941)	Syntax	415 (400)
Student life	370	specific languages	T.4–5
Study and teaching		Syria	T.2–5691
education	370	Systems analysis	003 (004)
specific subjects	T.1–07	Systems engineering	620.7 (620)

T

Table service	642 (641)
Tactics (Military)	355
Tagalog language	499.2
	(400 / 499.2)
Tailoring	
commerical	687 (680)
domestic	646.4 (646.2)
Taiwan	T.2–51
Tales	
customs	398
specific literatures	T.3–3
Talmud	296.2
	(290 / 296.2)
Tamil language	494 (400 / 494)
Tamil Nadu (India)	T.2–548
Tanganyika	T.2–678
Tanzania	T.2–678
Taoism	299 (290 / 299)
Tapestries	746.3 (746)
Tapirs	599.72
	(591/599.72)
Tariffs	
commerce	382 (380.1)
law	343 (340)
Tasmania (Australia)	T.2–946
Taste	612.87 (612)
Tatting	746.43 (746)
Taxation	
economics	335 (330)
law	343 (340)
Tayside (Scotland)	T.2–412
Teaching	371.3
Teaching aids	371.32 (370)
Teaching materials	371.32 (370)
Teaching methods	371.3
Technical drawing	604.2 (604)
Technological	
innovations	
economics	330
technology	600
Technology	600
Teeth	
diseases	617.6 (610)
physiology	612
Telecommunication	384
Telephones	
communications	384.6 (384)
engineering	621.38
Telescopes	522 (520)
Television	
communications	384.5
engineering	621.388
	(621.38)
entertainment	791.45 (791)
music	781.5 (781)
photography	778.5 (770)
Telugu	494 (400 / 494)

Temperance	363.4
ethics	178 (170)
Temperate zones	T.2–12
Temperature	536
Tenerife (Spain)	T.2–649
Tennessee (U.S.A.)	T.2–76
Tennis, Lawn	796.342
	(796 / 796.342)
Terminals (Air transport)	387.73 (387.7)
Terminals (Water transport)	387.1 (387)
Terrorism	
criminology	364
social welfare	363.3
Tertiary education	378 (370)
Teutonic languages	430 (400 / 430)
Texas (U.S.A.)	T.2–764
Textiles	
arts	746
painting	746.6 (746)
technology	677 (670)
Thailand	T.2–593
Thallophyta	588 (581 / 588)
Thames River (England)	T.2–423
Theatre	792
Theatre music	781.5 (781)
Theism	210 (200)
Theology	200
Therapeutic systems	615.5 (610)
Thermodynamics	536
Thermoelectricity	537.6 (537)
Third Republic	944.081 (944)
Thought and thinking	153 (150)
Tibet	T.2–51
Tibetan language	495 (400 / 495)
Ticks	595 (591/595)
Tides	525 (520)
Timber	
pulp technology	676 (670)
technology	674 (670)
Time measurment	529
Tissue	
biology	574.8 (574)
botany	581.8 (580)
zoology	591.8 (591)
Titles (Form of address)	929.7 (529)
Toads	597.6
	(591 / 597.6)
Tobacco consumption	
addiction	613.8 (613)
ethics	178 (170)
social customs	394 (390)
social welfare	362.29 (362)
Tobago	T.2–7298
Togo	T.2–66
Tools, Hand	621.9
Tools, Machine	621.8
Topology	514
Torrid zones	T.2–13

Torts	346 (340)
Totalitarianism	321 (320)
Toucans	598.7
	(591/598.7)
Touch	612.88 (612)
Tourism	338.4 (338)
Town and country planning	711 (710)
Towns	
sociology	306.76 (306)
Toxicology	615.9 (610)
Toy theatres	791.5 (791)
Toys	
childcare	649.1 (649)
games	790.1
handicrafts	745.592
	(745/745.592)
manufacture	688 (680)
social customs	394 (390)
Track athletics	796.42
	(796/796.42)
Trade	380.1
Trade agreements	382 (380.1)
Trade catalogues	T.1–029
Trade unions	331.88 (331)
Traffic control equipment	625.7
Traffic safety	363.125
Tragedies (Drama)	
literature	800
specific literatures	T.3–2
performing arts	792.1 (792)
Transkei (South Africa)	T.2–6879
Transplantation of organs	617 (610)
Transportation	380.5
engineering	625.7
Transportation, Air	387.7
safety	363.124 (363.1)
Transportation, Land	388
safety	363.125
Transportation, Space	387.8 (387.7)
safety	363.124
	(363.1)
Transportation, Urban	388.4
Transportation, Water	387
safety	363.123
Transvaal (South Africa)	T.2–682
Trapping	
animal husbandry	639
sport	799 (796/799)
Travel	910
See also specific places	
Trees	
botany	582.16
	(580/582.16)
forestry	634.9
Trials	340
Tribes	306
Trigonometry	516

Trinidad and Tobago	T.2–7298
Trinitarian doctrine	
(Christianity)	231 (230)
Tripura (India)	T.2–541
Trombones	
music	788 (784/788)
Tropics	T.2–13
Trumpets	
music	788 (784/788)
Tubas	
music	788 (784/788)
Tubulidentata	599.7
	(591/599.7)
Tudor dynasty	942.05 (941)
Tunisia	T.2–611
Turkey	T.2–561
Turkeys	
animal husbandry	636.5 (636)
zoology	598.6
	(591/598.6)
Turkish language	494 (400/494)
Turtles	
zoology	597.9
	(591/597.9)
Tyne and Wear	
(England)	T.2–428
Typewriting	652 (651)
Tyrone (N. Ireland)	T.2–4162

U

UFOs	001.9 (001)
U.S.A. See United States of America	
USSR See Union of Soviet Socialist Republics	
Uganda	T.2–6761
Ulster (Ireland)	T.2–416
See also Northern Ireland, British Isles, United Kingdom	
Ultrasonics	534
Ultraviolet rays	535.8 (535)
Underdeveloped areas	T.2–17
Underground railway	
urban transportation	388.4
Unemployed	331.1 (331)
Unguiculata	599.3
	(591/599.3)
Union of Soviet Socialist Republics	T.2–47
Unitarianism	288 (280/288)
United Arab Emirates	T.2–53
United Kingdom	
area number	T.2–41
history	941
See also British Isles	
United Nations	341.23 (340)
United Reformed Church	285 (280/285)

United States of America
  area number   T.2–73
  history   973
  painters   759.1 (750)
  philosophers   191 (100)
Universe   523.1 (520)
Universal languages   499.9
                   (400/499.9)
Universities   378 (370)
Upper Volta   T.2–66
Ural-Altaic languages   494 (400/494)
Urban areas   T.2–1732
Urban communities   307.6 (307)
Urban renewal   307
Urban transportation   388.4 (388)
Urdu language   491.44
                   (400/491.44)
Urinary system
  diseases   616.6
                   (610/616.6)
  physiology   612.4 (612)
Uruguay   T.2–895
Usage (Language)
  specific languages   T.4–8
Utah (U.S.A.)   T.2–79
Uttar Pradesh (India)   T.2–542
Utilities
  buildings   696 (690)
  home economics   644 (640)
  public provision   363.3

V

Vacuum technology   621.5
Valleys   T.2–144
Vanishing animals   591.04
Vanuatu   T.2–932
Variety shows   792.7 (792)
Varnishing   667 (660)
Vaudeville   792.7 (792)
Vegetables
  agriculture   635
Vehicles
  aircraft   629.1
  automobiles   629.2
  vessels   623.8
Vehicular transportation
  (Ground)   388.3 (388)
Venda (South Africa) T.2–6829
Venereal disease   616.6 (610)
Venezuela   T.2–87
Ventilation   697 (690)
Ventriloquism   793.8
               (793/793.8)
Vermont (U.S.A.)   T.2–74
Vertebrates   596 (591/596)
Vessels (Nautical)
  naval engineering   623.8
  transportation   387.2 (387)

Veterans (Ex-service
  personnel)
  social welfare   362.8 (362)
Veterinary medicine 636.089 (636)
Vibrations
  engineering   620.3 (620)
  physics   534
Vices
  Christianity   241 (230)
  ethics   170
Victims of crime   362.8 (362)
Victoria (Australia) T.2–945
Video tapes   T.1–0208
Vietnam   T.2–597
Villages   307.72 (307)
Violas
  music   787 (784/787)
Violence control   363.4
Violins
  music   787.2
             (784/787.2)
Viral diseases   616.9 (610)
Virgin Islands   T.2–7297
Virginia (U.S.A.)   T.2–75
Virtues and vices
  Christianity   241 (230)
  ethics   170
Vision   612.84 (612)
Visual education   700
Visually handicapped
  persons
  medical aspects   617.7 (610)
  social welfare   362.41 (362)
Vital statistics   304.6 (304)
Vitamins   613.2 (613)
Vivaria   574.07
  botany   580.7
  zoology   590.7
Vocabulary   T.4–3
Vocal music   782
Vocational education 373 (370)
Vocational guidance 371.4
Voice (Music)   783
Voice (Speaking) 808.5 (808)
Volcanoes   551.2 (551)
Volleyball   796.32
            (796/796.32)
Voluntary associations 366
  social welfare   361.7 (361)
Voting   324 (320)
Voyages and travels 910
Vultures   598.9
            (591/598.9)

W

Wages   331.1 (331)
Waldensian Church 284 (280/284)

Wales
  area number   T.2–429
  history   942.9
  See also British Isles,
    United Kingdom
Walking (Sport)   796.51
      (796 / 796.51)
Wallabies   599.1
      (591/599.1)
Walruses   599.74
      (591 / 599.74)
Walvis Bay (South
  Africa)   T.2–688
War
  diplomacy   327 (320)
  ethics   172 (170)
  law   341 (340)
  military science   355
  sociology   303.6 (303)
Warm-blooded vertebrates   599 (591 / 599)
Warships
  military science   359 (355)
  technology   623.8
Warwickshire
  (England)   T.2–424
Washington, D.C.
  (U.S.A.)   T.2–753
Washington (State)
  U.S.A.   T.2–79
Waste disposal
  social services   363.72 (363.7)
Waste technology   604.6 (604)
Water
  hydrology   551
Water birds   598.3
      (591 / 598.3)
Water life
  biology   574.92 (574)
Water skiing   797.3
      (796 / 797.3)
Water supply
  building   697 (690)
  economics   333.9 (333)
  hydraulic engineering   627
  hydraulic power   621.2
    engineering
  public utilities   363.61 (363.6)
Water transportation   387
  safety   363.123
Waxes
  chemical technology   665 (660)
Weaponry
  arms and armour   739.7 (730)
  military science   355
  technology   623.4 (623)
Weather   551.6
Weathering (Physical
  geology)   551.3 (551)

Weaving
  arts   746.41 (746)
  textile technology   677 (670)
Weddings
  customs   392 (390)
  etiquette   395
Welfare, Social   361
Welfare state   361.6 (361)
Wellington (City) New
  Zealand   T.2–93127
Welsh language   491.66
      (400 / 491.66)
West Africa   T.2–66
West Bengal (India)   T.2–541
West Germany   T.2–43
West Indies   T.2–729
West Midlands (County)
  England   T.2–424
West Sussex (England)   T.2–422
West Virginia (U.S.A.)   T.2–75
West Yorkshire (County)
  England   T.2–428
Western Australia   T.2–941
Western Hemisphere   T.2–1812
Western Isles
  (Scotland)   T.2–4111
Western philosophy   190 (100)
Westminster Catechism   238 (230)
Whales
  animal husbandry   639.2 (639)
  zoology   599.5
      (591 / 599.5)
Wheat
  crop   633
  plant   584 (580 / 584)
Wheel
  physics   531
Whist   795.41
      (793 / 795.41)
White collar crimes   364
Wholesaling   658.8
Wight, Isle of (England)   T.2–422
Wildlife conservation   639.9 (639)
Wildlife parks   574.07
  botany   580.7
  zoology   590.7
Wiltshire (England)   T.2–423
Wind band   784.8
      (784 / 784.8)
Wind instruments
  music   788 (784 / 788)
Windward Islands   T.2–7298
Winter Olympics   796.98
      (796 / 796.98)
Winter sports   796.9
      (796 / 796.9)
Wireless *See* Radio
Wisconsin (U.S.A.)   T.2–77

Wit and humour
  collections   808.87 (808)
  composition   808.7 (808)
  criticism   809.7 (809)
  specific literatures   T.3–7
Witchcraft
  folklore   398
  occultism   133.4 (130)
Witness bearing
  Christianity   248 (230)
Women
  diseases   618.1 (610)
  education   376 (370)
  social welfare   362.8 (362)
  sociology   305.3 (305)
Women's voices (Music) 782.6 (782)
Wood
  carpentry   694 (690)
  carving   736
  handicrafts   745.51
                  (745 / 745.51)
  technology   676 (670)
Wood pulp   676 (670)
Woodwind instruments
  music   788 (784 / 788)
Woody plants   582 (580 / 582)
Worcester (England) T.2–424
Word games   793.7
                  (793 / 793.7)
Work study
  management   658.5 (658)
Workers' guilds   331.88 (331)
World community
  organizations   341.2 (340)
World history   909 (900)
World politics   327 (320)
World War 1   940.3 (940)
World War 2   940.53 (940)
Worship   200
Wounds   617.1 (610)
Wrestling   796.8
                (796 / 796.8)
Writing (Manual)   411 (400)
  office work   652 (651)
Writing (Literary)   800
Wyoming (U.S.A.)   T.2–78

X

X-rays
  physics   539.7 (539)

Xylophones
  music   786.8
                (784 / 786.8)

Y

YMCA   267 (230)
YWCA   267 (230)
Yachting   797.1
                (796 / 797.1)
Yemen Arab Republic T.2–53
Yemen People's
  Republic   T.2–53
Yiddish literature   839.09
                (800/839.09)
Yom Kippur   296.3
                (290 / 296.3)
Yorkshire (England) T.2–428
Yoruba language   496 (400 / 496)
Young people
  psychology   155 (150)
  sociology   305.2 (305)
Youth
  culture   305.2 (305)
  social welfare   362.7 (362)
Yugoslavia   T.2–497

Z

Zaire   T.2–67
Zambia   T.2–6894
Zebras   599.725
                (591 / 599.725)
Zen Buddhism   294.39
                (290 / 294.39)
Zimbabwe   T.2–6891
Zionism   320
Zithers
  music   787 (784 / 787)
Zodiac
  astrology   133.5 (130)
  astronomy   523 (520)
Zodiacal light   523.5 (520)
Zoological sciences 590
Zoology   591
Zoos   590.7
Zoroastrian religion 295 (290 / 295)
Zulu language   496 (400 / 496)
Zululand (South Africa) T.2–6849